SURVIVING A
BORDERLINE
PARENT

How to Heal Your Childhood
Wounds & Build Trust,
Boundaries, and Self-Esteem

KIMBERLEE ROTH and
FREDA B. FRIEDMAN, PH.D., LCSW
Foreword by RANDI KREGER

New Harbinger Publications, Inc.

Publisher's Note

This publication is designed to provide accurate and authoritative information in regard to the subject matter covered. It is sold with the understanding that the publisher is not engaged in rendering psychological, financial, legal, or other professional services. If expert assistance or counseling is needed, the services of a competent professional should be sought.

Distributed in Canada by Raincoast Books

Copyright © 2003 by Kimberlee Roth and Freda B. Friedman
New Harbinger Publications, Inc.
5674 Shattuck Avenue
Oakland, CA 94609

Cover design by Amy Shoup
Text design by Michele Waters

ISBN-13 978-1-57224-328-6
ISBN-10 1-57224-328-7

Printed in the United States of America

New Harbinger Publications' website address: www.newharbinger.com

10   09   08

15   14   13   12   11   10   9

Contents

Foreword

Since I began researching and writing *Stop Walking on Eggshells* in the mid-1990s, I've interacted with thousands of people who care about a friend or family member with borderline personality disorder, or BPD.

While all people with a borderline loved one need validation, insight, and coping skills, the people closest to my heart have been those who were parented by someone with BPD. If coping with BPD behaviors is difficult, being raised by someone with an uncontrolled, unacknowledged, or untreated pervasive personality disorder can be emotionally devastating.

Again and again, children of parents with BPD say the same things:

"I wonder what it would be like to feel 'normal.'"

"It makes me feel uncomfortable when people treat me well, but I'm not sure why."

"When I see a parent soothing a child in a loving way, I feel like crying."

"People always end up hurting me, just when I've made myself vulnerable to them."

"I feel like pieces of a jigsaw puzzle. I would put myself together, but I don't know what piece fits where and I have no idea what the whole picture looks like."

"I feel physically sick when the phone rings and I think it may be my borderline parent."

"When I allow myself to really feel, I find myself wondering *what's wrong with me?*"

If the previous statements sound familiar, your parent or guardian may have BPD. If so, what you're feeling is a *normal reaction*. You're not alone—millions of people just like you are coping with a less-than-ideal childhood and struggling to become the person they were meant to be.

Unlike you, however, they probably don't have a name for what they experienced growing up. Thanks to this book, you do. That knowledge gives you the power to understand why your parent acted the way he or she did, how it affected you, and how to now become the person you really want to be.

Borderline personality disorder is not an easy condition to describe. In *Stop Walking on Eggshells*, my coauthor Paul Mason and I take two chapters to describe BPD: one to give the formal definition and one to explain how it unfolds in the real world.

To complicate matters, people with BPD experience the disorder in different ways. Some of them make excellent parents. Others do not. Since you're reading this book, it's likely that your borderline parent:

◇ was so intent on getting her own needs met that she couldn't take care of yours—or perhaps even differentiate her needs from yours

◇ looked to you to provide him with unconditional love rather than the other way around

◇ either emotionally abandoned you or smothered and controlled you, leading to feelings of worthlessness, shame, and rage

◇ made you feel that she only loved you for what you could achieve, not who you were

◇ had unpredictable moods, alternating between loving and cruel words and actions.

With the help of this book, you'll be able to really see what happened to you, how it affected you then, and how it continues to affect you now, even if you no longer interact with your parent by choice or because your parent has passed away.

You'll gain insight into why you don't feel normal—because our culture promotes the idea of unconditional parental love, and the love you received seemed to be inconsistent and conditional.

You'll be able to understand why it makes you feel uncomfortable when people treat you well—because you've learned that it will be followed, sooner or later, by disappointment and betrayal.

You'll now know why you cry when you see a parent soothing a child in a loving way—because it reminds you of the love you felt like you never received and perhaps felt you were not worthy enough to receive.

You'll realize why you believe that people always hurt you in the end—because that's what you've come to expect. It becomes a certainty in an uncertain world, leading to a kind of dysfunctional comfort in which the pain you know is preferable to the unknown, *even if the unknown is supposed to be better.*

And finally, you'll gain insight into why you don't know who you really are—because you may have served as the container for your parent's pain, rage, and projections. You keep going back to the parent to get the love you so desperately need, only to feel betrayed when your impossible expectations are dashed once more.

Whatever your age, it's never too late to get off the emotional roller coaster. With the help of an understanding clinician and this book, you can piece together what happened to you, understand the choices you've made so far, and determine where you want to go from here. Who do you want to be? Can you finally accept that you can't get much of what you need from your parent, and learn how to give it to yourself or get it from others?

It's risky to try. But it's just as risky to leave things the way they are. You won't be alone on this journey. Rest assured that others have taken the trip, and they've found the destination worth it. You will too.

—Randi Kreger
   Coauthor, *Stop Walking on Eggshells*
   Author, *The Stop Walking on Eggshells Workbook*
   Owner of the Welcome to Oz Internet Support Groups
   Owner of BPD Central at www.BPDCentral.com
   Board of Directors, Personality Disorders Awareness Network

Preface

You may be picking up this book out of curiosity or interest because you have a parent or relative who is "difficult." So difficult that at times, it may feel like you're walking on eggshells—or even worse, on land mines that might explode at any time. So difficult that at times it may feel like this person is almost impossible to please or to understand, to tolerate or to love, but also incredibly difficult to walk away from. And having a parent like this very likely has had an impact on how you feel about yourself.

Everyone can be difficult at times. Don't confuse that with the label of "difficult" that is often applied to a condition known in the field of psychology and psychiatry as *borderline personality disorder,* or BPD. Many therapy clients Freda Friedman has worked with over the past twenty years have been termed "difficult" in all sorts of ways by their children, spouses, friends, coworkers, and even their therapists. People with this disorder, or even with just some of the symptoms, can be charming, brilliant, creative, empathic, delightful, and, yes, difficult. They can also be highly sensitive, have difficulty understanding their feelings, and possess few skills to manage their emotions. This may, in turn, cause them to use a variety of defensive strategies in order to feel better, strategies that to others may make them seem, well, difficult.

The impact of these symptoms on the person who has them is often enormous and challenging, as it is for family and friends as well. Unfortunately, though there have been numerous books and articles published and conferences held about BPD in recent years, few have addressed the particular issues faced by children of a parent with borderline personality disorder. This book speaks to the large numbers of people whose parents have diagnosed or undiagnosed symptoms that fall along the BPD spectrum.

As you read this book, many of the discussions and examples will jump out at you and sound eerily familiar. There will probably also be sections of this book that don't ring quite true for you. That doesn't mean this book isn't for you. What it means is that BPD presents itself in many different ways at different times under different circumstances. What it means is that people with BPD may behave, particularly with loved ones, in ways that often are variable and confusing. That's part of the problem for everyone involved—there's no straight path for parent, adult child, or anyone else involved in the problems associated with BPD.

Although the experience of having a parent with this disorder or its symptoms is intensely personal, there are some fairly typical stages adult children will likely go through as they start to understand their circumstances and reactions; these stages include denial, despair, anger, acceptance, and hopefully, some sense of resolution. But they certainly don't move in a linear way. Your emotions may seesaw; overwhelming feelings may pass and then return. Just when you think you're "over it," some image, comment, or interaction may send you back into emotional turmoil. It's like rock scrambling in the rain: one step forward, sometimes half a step—or two—back. It's a journey that may last a long time and, even then, never really seem to end. It often helps adult children to know that they aren't alone in their confusion, frustration, or pain, and that things can improve as you cope, learn, and continue to grow.

It's sometimes hard to be compassionate and optimistic about the possibility of change. It's important though, as you're reading this book, to set realistic goals for yourself, keep an open mind, avoid always-or-never ways of thinking, and be patient with yourself.

We've included insights from numerous sources in this book, including Marsha Linehan, Ph.D., who pioneered the development of dialectical behavioral therapy (DBT), a well-recognized and commonly used method of cognitive therapy for the treatment of BPD. It's an approach to treatment that Freda (along with thousands of other clinicians) has found extremely helpful and effective in her work with patients and their families. We've also developed much original material to provide you with a range of techniques and tools to practice and to think about.

The process of writing this book was a collaborative one. Kimberlee, a writer, conceived of the idea, conducted interviews with clinicians and adult children of parents with BPD symptoms, and composed much of the text. Freda served as clinical advisor, contributing her professional knowledge as well as several sections of the book, all based on her years of therapeutic practice with those showing BPD traits and their family members. At times we interpreted the material in different ways, and so we tried to present the multiple facets of the picture to readers—not an easy thing to do when the feelings and beliefs of everyone involved are quite strong and, at times, seemingly at odds. That said, the book is written from the perspective of grown children of challenging parents. Parents themselves were not interviewed, but their perspective is generally reflected in Freda's insights based on her clinical work.

In some of the cases we came across, BPD was formally diagnosed in the parent by a clinician. In other cases, the adult child, and/or his or her therapist, strongly suspect BPD is or was involved. It's critically important that, as you read this book, you not "diagnose" someone who you believe has BPD. You may read and realize that the symptoms and circumstances we describe fit your parent and your situation very closely (and so we expect that the tools contained herein will prove helpful to you). However, diagnosis of the disorder per se must be left to a qualified professional; the experiences related by those interviewed are by no means exclusive to BPD. They occur in many, many families, including those with a parent—or parents—who is depressed, anxious, traumatized, alcohol- or substance-abusing, or who suffers from another personality disorder or mental illness.

So why did we write a book specifically about the potential effects of BPD on adult children? Because even with the stigma attached to the other mental health issues just listed, there seems to be more recognition of them by professionals and therefore more treatment, at least at this point in time. And with recognition and treatment come an "explanation" that makes it somewhat easier for loved ones to face the associated problems.

With best wishes for the challenges, changes, and rewards that lie ahead.

Acknowledgments

There are dozens of names missing from the cover of this book, names of those who contributed in tremendous ways—this could not have been done without them. Scott Edelstein, my agent, shared his energy, talent, sensitivity, and an uncanny knack for knowing precisely when to leave encouraging voicemail messages. He is a true gift to an author. I am indebted to Freda for helping me take an idea, inspired by a newspaper article that I wrote about BPD, and turn it into the book you're holding. She saw my (rough) vision and, right from the start, made valuable suggestions, offered constructive yet gentle critiques, and shared her professional experience, always with passion and compassion (I know, I know, *always* is rarely true, but in this case it is!). She's been an inspiring mentor, a willing therapist-on-call, and has come to be a close friend. Randi blazed a trail and has made life immeasurably easier for those that follow. Bethanne, Kellye, Debbie, Barbara, and Steve provided never-ending and unconditional support and friendship. Louise, keen insight; Running Man, a listening ear and enthusiastic fanning of writing aspirations that day on the beach; my parents, each in their own ways and times, encouragement to put pen to paper. Finally, without all of those who shared their time, their knowledge, and their personal stories with a virtual stranger in order to help others, this book would—could—not be. Thank you. Thank you. Thank you.

—K.R.

First, to Kim, my coauthor, who has been a wonderful inspiration and an ideal mixture of diligence, humor, and compassion. To my teachers, mentors, supervisors, and many colleagues, especially at New York Hospital-Cornell Medical School and at The Phoenix Institute, a big thank-you for giving me lessons in caring, compassion, and the highest standards of professionalism in this work that has come to mean so much to me. To my DBT colleagues everywhere, especially Drs. Marsha Linehan, Cindy Sanderson, and Charlie Swenson, a huge debt of gratitude for inspiring me and teaching me the dialectics of life. And most of all, to my clients in New York and Chicago, the biggest note of gratitude and appreciation for sharing with me your struggles, showing me what courage really means and for all your hope, perseverance, and willingness to take the hard road to growth. And, lastly, my thanks and appreciation to Harvey for his never-ending feedback, ideas, encouragement, and computer skills.

—F.F.

Introduction

As a child, did you feel like you fell short, disappointing a parent, stepparent, or caretaker because you weren't good enough, didn't do enough, or just weren't able to please, no matter how hard you tried? Did you feel responsible for your parent's happiness and guilty if you felt happy yourself? Did you feel damned if you did and damned if you didn't, that whatever you did or said was the wrong thing (and boy would you pay for it)? Were you accused of things you hadn't done? Did you feel manipulated at times? Feel appreciated one minute and attacked the next? Thought you must be "crazy" because a parent's actions or reactions didn't make any sense? Question your own intuition, judgment, or memory, believing you must have missed or misinterpreted something? Did you feel on guard all the time, that life with your parent was never predictable?

You weren't crazy. Not then, and not now, though it may still feel that way. What felt crazy-making to you may well have been being parented by someone who had traits of borderline personality disorder.

Though relatively common, borderline personality disorder is often overlooked or misdiagnosed by therapists and clinicians and denied by those who suffer from it. It's a confusing, complex disorder that's extremely difficult for all involved: for the person with BPD, for the clinicians trying to understand and help their client, and perhaps most of all, for the children who have to endure its unpredictable effects.

No one chooses their parents and, as young children, once you're brought into this world, you're not in a position to opt out of your relationship with them. In fact, you desperately need them—to provide food and shelter, to prompt you to learn, to model ways to interact in society, to nurture you, to show you affection, and to provide unconditional love. A parent with BPD, however, may not have been able to consistently provide all of these things to you, through no fault or deficit of yours. They may not have received that kind of care themselves. It may seem ironic, but your parent may actually have consciously or unconsciously reinforced *you* as the caretaker to meet his or her needs, to be the nurturer and provider of emotional support, even though you were a young child.

Does This Sound Familiar?

Which of the following match your experience with a parent or other caretaker growing up?

_____ Your parent teased you, often cruelly, about physical attributes, mental abilities, intelligence, habits, or other personal characteristics.

_____ You remember sequences of events and conversations differently from your parent.

_____ Your parent confided in you, perhaps with inappropriate details, and expected you to keep his secret or to side with her.

_____ You were treated like a little adult instead of a child, expected to consistently assume responsibilities parents should, such as emotionally comforting or reassuring your parent, frequently cooking, cleaning, caring for siblings, and other responsibilities.

_____ Your feelings were discounted, denied, criticized, or ignored.

_____ You weren't permitted to express strong emotions, particularly anger.

_____ You didn't receive much physical or emotional affection—hugs, kisses, or being told you were loved.

_____ You were held to extremely high, often unattainable standards, and those standards shifted so you had a hard time knowing what was expected of you.

_____ You were given mixed messages about your appearance or your behavior.

_____ You weren't encouraged to explore, experiment, or develop your own opinions.

_____ Your privacy and/or your belongings weren't respected.

While you were growing up, did you feel

____ scared?

____ confused?

____ angry?

____ guilty?

____ responsible?

____ far older than your age and your peers?

____ listless?

____ invisible?

____ unlovable?

Now as an adult, do you

____ find yourself in abusive, unfulfilling, or unhealthy relationships?

____ feel unable to trust others and let your guard down?

____ expect the worst from others—family, friends, and strangers?

____ feel responsible for others' moods, feelings, and actions?

____ put others' needs ahead of your own?

____ have a hard time knowing what you want?

____ tend not to trust your own feelings and reactions?

____ feel uneasy with success or have difficulty simply enjoying life?

____ get highly anxious in social settings or new situations?

____ fear taking risks, especially where relationships are concerned?

____ hold yourself to standards nearing perfection?

____ feel worthless, hopeless, or depressed?

If you relate to many of these experiences, chances are you may have been raised by a parent with BPD or BPD-like traits. Chances are also good that the effects are still with you, in subtle, and likely fundamental, ways. They probably have affected and continue to affect who you are, as well as your relationships with others—how you choose and who you choose to spend time with, to befriend, to partner with, to love.

A New Reality

This isn't another book focused on family dysfunction or about terrible mothers (though BPD is diagnosed in women three times as often as in men, for a variety of reasons we'll cover shortly). It's not about blame or wallowing either—you are all molded by so much more than a dysfunctional past, and you must ultimately take responsibility for creating the life you want. Certainly, it's important to acknowledge and identify the effects of BPD on your life. It's equally important to realize that it neither dictates who you are nor fixes your destiny.

This book is really about just two things: understanding and change. We hope it will help validate your experience as a child of a borderline parent, help you identify the impact it had and continues to have on you, regardless of whether your parent is still alive, and that it will lead you to more positive alternatives to the negative thoughts, beliefs, feelings, and behaviors you may have learned. We also hope reading this book will help you envision—and cultivate—the *you* you want to be and begin to build the future you want to live. It may sound like a cliché, but it's true: you deserve to be happy.

As an adult child of someone with BPD, you've likely been cultivating and honing certain beliefs and behaviors since infancy. Though you may not remember, as a baby, you viscerally sensed anger, frustration, and despair through your parents' touch, voice, and breathing rhythm; you felt tension tightening the air. Growing up in continual response to erratic and intense emotions has taught you reflexive responses, which come as instantly as your leg jerks when the doctor taps your knee with a rubber mallet or you spin around when someone calls your name. Well- and long-ingrained, what you learned may have helped you protect yourself physically, mentally, and emotionally from your borderline parent, but it's probably not serving you well now—in fact, it may be keeping you from fully understanding and accepting yourself, and from connecting with others. The catch is, your coping mechanisms and ways of relating to your self and to others are so much a part of your emotional repertoire, you rarely stop to question them. They define your worldview, like the tint of glass lenses, and therefore dictate how you see and interact with the world.

This book assumes that you're thinking about making some positive changes in your life. It presupposes that you have an inkling that there's more to life than what you've long thought, been told, or have been living with in your family of origin. It presupposes that you want to pursue that sense of possibility, frightening though it may be. Regardless of where you're at emotionally, this book assumes *potential* and your willingness—and courage—to reach for it.

How do you begin to take a hard look at your life, without the tint of your old lenses? How can you come to know and trust yourself and dismantle the defenses that may surround you? How do you begin to conceive of a new and better life? How do you learn to see the good in people, to feel deserving of healthy relationships and a full, rewarding life? This book will help you start to explore the many ways. You'll make the changes you choose to make at your own pace. The rewards—though they come slowly and quietly—are great.

In the past few years, there have been several excellent books written about BPD. A trip to your local library or bookstore today yields an armful of titles that weren't available even ten years ago to both individuals with the disorder and their loved ones. There are also numerous Web sites, chat rooms, listservs and other online resources available. Other than giving some history and an overview of BPD in the first chapter, we don't repeat work that's already been done, but rather have tried to use all that's come before as a springboard for further exploration.

How to Use This Book

If this is the first time you're hearing of borderline personality disorder or you've heard the term and want to know more, chapter 1 spells out the signs and symptoms of the disorder and explains how those behaviors can affect children.

If you're familiar with the traits and behaviors of BPD and recognize one or more of your parents, stepparents, or caretakers as having had the disorder, you may want to just scan chapter 1. Then move on to chapter 2 to see how the messages you received as a child may still be influencing you now. If you're a partner, friend, or family member of someone whose parent has or had BPD, this book will provide insight into the experiences that shaped the person you know today.

Throughout the book, we'll use the term *adult child* to refer to adult children of a parent with borderline personality disorder. For ease of reading, we sometimes use the term *borderline parent* to refer to someone with BPD traits. The term parent may refer to stepparents, grandparents, or any other adult with primary child care responsibility.

You'll see many places throughout the book to "Stop and Think." These exercises are designed to help you apply the concepts in the text to your own particular circumstances and experiences. You may want to use a notebook or journal to record your responses and reactions. So you can measure your progress down the road, be sure to date all of your entries.

It's Not All in a Name

As you read, you may wonder if your parent really has BPD, if he or she has never been diagnosed by a professional. Your parent may have been diagnosed with another disorder such as major depression, schizophrenia, bipolar disorder (manic depression), or something else. Your parent may have substance abuse issues as well. BPD doesn't occur in a vacuum; it may exist alongside and together with other diagnoses. Furthermore, BPD is not always diagnosed since those with these traits may not seek help or, if they do seek help, clinicians may miss or misdiagnose the disorder. The bottom line is, you don't have to be a credentialed clinician to recognize troublesome and unhealthy behaviors. The label or diagnosis isn't the issue. If what you read resonates with your experience, and the exercises get you thinking about new ways to handle vexing belief systems and behaviors, we think you'll benefit, regardless of a formal diagnosis (or lack of one).

The stories you'll read in this book are based upon interviews and clinical experience with adult children and other family members. In talking with adult children, we found their experiences to be strikingly similar. Symptoms of BPD can ricochet between extremes—raging or being unable to express anger, idealization or devaluation of others—making the disorder especially tricky for clinicians to diagnose. Still, adult children find that they share nearly identical experiences at times, and can in fact identify very typical borderline behavior.

The remarkable similarities in how the behaviors are observed, experienced, and remembered have allowed us to create composite stories. We have also changed the names and specific identifying traits and circumstances of individuals, to protect the privacy of those interviewed and their families, while not compromising the power of their accounts.

PART 1

The Past

CHAPTER 1

I Never Knew It
Had a Name

"Yes, but what *is* it?" people often ask upon hearing the term *borderline personality disorder*. Characterized in large part by the inability to regulate, or manage, emotions and a deep-seated fear of abandonment, the disorder is one of the least researched and understood, though that is beginning to change, thanks to increased awareness, the birth of several advocacy organizations, and increased funding opportunities for clinical research.

Those three little letters—B-P-D—often elicit a roll of the eyes among practitioners. Because of its heterogeneous symptoms and wide spectrum of severity, many have trouble diagnosing BPD. Once they do, some aren't sure how to treat it, and given the disorder's complexity, many are hesitant to.

The Silent Treatment

We don't see or hear much about BPD in the media, which is surprising given the number of Americans who suffer from the disorder—and a source of continual frustration to family members in search of information and validation of their experience. Borderline personality disorder afflicts about 2 percent of the population, or some six million people (Swartz et al. 1990). When you tally the partners and children, parents and siblings, and friends and coworkers, the number who are affected on a daily basis quickly rises to thirty million or more. Still, women's magazines bombard us with tips for everything from firm breasts to fluffy soufflés, raising smart kids to dressing for success, and men's magazines proffer analogous advice for maintaining a tumescent member, parenting, accessing your true feelings, even cooking. But no one says much about BPD.

Perhaps one reason for the silence around BPD is there's no wonder drug or quick fix, making it a long, winding road to recovery and to a potentially happy ending. It's difficult to explain BPD in snappy headlines and sound bites to a restless audience wont to channel surf.

"Even when I speak to groups of clinicians, it takes me thirty minutes to describe what BPD is so that they understand. You just can't do that on television," says Randi Kreger (2001). And no celebrity has stepped forward to tell of their personal struggle with the disorder. In fact, most of the celebrities that have been associated with BPD generally live in infamy: Joan Crawford (a.k.a. Mommie Dearest), Marilyn Monroe, and Vincent Van Gogh. It's probably safe to say it's not a highly sought claim to fame.

As a result of the silence around BPD, adult children are frequently relieved to the point of tears upon reading a detailed description of the disorder for the first time. It gives their confusing and contradictory childhood experience a name, an explanation, and most importantly, validation. "I thought *I* was crazy"; "I always knew something wasn't right, but I had no idea what it was"; "It was all I knew, so it seemed normal"; "As kids, we walked on eggshells, but I didn't know that others didn't" are some common reactions.

People with borderline personality disorder can act in incongruous and inconsistent ways, yet, at times, appear so perfectly normal, reasonable, rational, and sure of themselves in the process that those around them are left to wonder at their own sanity and perception of reality. Likewise, when people with BPD "act out" or rage, they can be so convinced of the appropriateness of and justification for the outburst that loved ones again question their take on reality, and what they must have done to set the spiral in motion. What a sense of relief to learn there was an explanation, and it wasn't something you caused!

Gender Inequity

BPD is often mentioned as a consequence of sexual abuse, which historically seemed to explain why women were diagnosed more often than men. There is certainly a correlation, according to many studies, but a simple and direct association is an oversimplification, and does not take into account factors such as the nature and severity of abuse; other types of trauma and neglect also enter into the picture.

In addition, in *Stop Walking on Eggshells*, Kreger and Mason (1998) list additional reasons why the incidence of BPD may be higher among women, including women receive more invalidating and inconsistent messages in this society than men, and women are socialized to be more dependent on others and therefore are more sensitive to rejection. Kreger and Mason also point out that the number of men with BPD may be higher than statistics would indicate. They point out that men are less likely to seek psychiatric help if they have a problem, so problems go undiagnosed. Furthermore, clinicians tend to recognize BPD more often in women, even when patient profiles are otherwise the same.

A Long Way to Recovery

BPD is extremely difficult, but not impossible, to cure. Those with BPD can improve, though it can take years. Medication, particularly anti-anxiety and antidepressant, coupled with therapy is most often employed. Among so-called higher-functioning borderlines, it's tougher to estimate improvement, given the inherent denial that often accompanies BPD.

One of the more common therapeutic approaches for BPD is dialectical behavior therapy (DBT), developed by Marsha Linehan, a Seattle-based psychologist who treats patients with BPD. Linehan explains DBT as "a little like the professional version of 'tough love'" (2001), with simultaneous expectations of change and acceptance of the individual as he is at that moment. Her method helps patients reconcile their polarized thinking, reframe cognitive distortions—that is, loosen up rigid thinking—manage extreme emotions, and apply healthier behaviors to the present issues in their lives. Therapists using DBT validate the borderline patient's reasons for relying on the dysfunctional behaviors ("when you rage, you're able to express your anger, and others agree to do what you want"), while working with them to find alternatives. While change can be slow, many patients learn that improvement is possible, and that there are alternate ways of seeing and interpreting what goes on around them.

Reading the Signs

The *DSM-IV-TR* (APA 2000) lists nine criteria, which clinicians use to diagnosis BPD. If patients meet any five or more of the observable symptoms, they are said to have the disorder. But there's a point of clarification: these traits must manifest themselves as a pervasive pattern. Nearly everyone at times could identify with the symptoms, though not to the same degree. In looking down the list, adult children will often say, "Oh, but I do that," or, "But that describes me too sometimes."

And they're probably right—to an extent. As Paul Shirley, MSW, coauthor of the *Stop Walking on Eggshells Workbook,* explains, "Most—if not all—mental illness is an exaggeration of some normal trait. Everybody goes back to check and make sure they've locked the door sometimes, but that does not mean everybody has an obsessive-compulsive disorder" (Shirley 2001). He cites the medical student syndrome in which students may start to recognize in themselves symptoms of the diseases they're studying. But exhibiting a behavior or occasionally having a negative thought, particularly one that isn't acted upon, does not a diagnosis make.

Keep in mind as you read the description of symptoms below that BPD involves a repeated pattern, likely played out consistently over the course of years, that interferes with healthy relationships and daily living. Adult children of parents with BPD may indeed demonstrate borderline-like behavior here and there—after all, that's what you were raised with—but this doesn't mean you have the disorder (if you have continued concerns that you do, contact a mental health professional).

Also keep in mind that while the criteria are set, at least until the next edition of the *DSM* is published by the American Psychiatric Association, symptoms play out in as many different ways as there are individuals with BPD—this in part is what makes the disorder so difficult to diagnose and so difficult for family members to understand. For instance, some adult children may recall hiding in a locked bathroom to wait out a parent's random, violent rages, while others may remember a parent who wouldn't tolerate or express anger at all. It's hard to believe such different behaviors are symptoms of the same disorder.

The Symptoms of BPD

After each criterion, taken from the *DSM-IV-TR* (APA 2000) and put into layperson's terms, explanations and vignettes follow to highlight the trait. We've also included *take-aways,* or the messages children are likely to receive from a parent exhibiting that trait.

1. Frantic attempts to prevent feelings of actual or perceived abandonment or rejection.

Owing to a poorly defined sense of self, people with BPD rely on others for their feelings of worth and emotional caretaking. So fearful are they of feeling alone that they may act in desperate ways that quite frequently bring about the very abandonment and rejection they're trying to avoid (and which therefore validates and reinforces their fears).

"Everyone jokes about having a horrible mother-in-law," says Rob, a thirty-nine-year-old son of a mother with BPD, "but I think my wife wins the prize. The week before we were to be married, while in a restaurant one evening, my mother picked a fight with Lisa. Then when she tried to defend herself, Mother called her a whore and dramatically stormed out the door. We ignored her angry phone messages for the next couple of days, and then two days before the wedding, we got a call from my aunt: Mother was in the hospital after attempting suicide."

The take-away for children may include the following:

◊ I can't leave (the house, the car, the relationship, etc.).

◊ It's my responsibility to stay with my parent.

◊ If I act differently (spend more time, do what she asks, say "I love you" more), she won't be so anxious or upset.

2. Patterns of relationships that are intense and unstable; repeated tendencies to shift between extremes of loving and hating another person.

Referred to as *splitting,* people with BPD have difficulty experiencing two feeling states at one time, or, for example, seeing a person's good and bad qualities simultaneously. They tend to see others as entirely good or entirely bad, as hero or villain, as ally or enemy, rather than see a person as generally good despite a few flaws. Sometimes they'll split siblings, believing one is the perfect child while another is nothing but trouble. Or, they might split the same person: one week (or day, or hour) the boss is the biggest sonofabitch around; the next week (or day, or hour) he's referred to as a trusted mentor and friend. Regardless of whether splitting, black-and-white or all-or-nothing thinking, occurs with one or more people, it may happen without provocation or even interaction.

Leanna couldn't seem to do anything right, according to her mother, Rita, who Leanna believes has BPD. Always the black sheep of the family, Leanna left home early, married young, and had a baby. Rita bad-mouthed her at every opportunity—to family, to friends, to coworkers, whoever would listen to the story of the supposedly unloving, irresponsible child—and wanted nothing to do with her granddaughter. Rita's son, Gene, was a different story. Though they'd sparred when he was in his teens, and he still dealt with alcoholism, Gene was the perfect son in his mother's eyes and sat high on a pedestal. When he'd forget her birthday, she'd excuse it by saying he was probably just busy; when he'd lose his jobs, she'd make a nasty comment about the poor management skills of his boss.

The take-aways may include:

◊ If I do such and such, I'll get back into the good graces of the mercurial parent.

◊ Things are either good or bad, black or white, all or nothing.

◊ People are heroes or, if they have some flaw, villains; allies or enemies.

◊ There's no gray area, no middle ground.

◊ I'm worshipped; if I continue to do what my parent wants, I'll continue to be the favorite.

◊ I'm despised. I need to try harder to be better so that I'll be worthy of being loved. Or, I'm worthless. Why even bother?

◊ One day I'm loved, the next day, hated—the world is an inconsistent place, and I have little control over what happens or how others treat me.

3. Difficulty describing the self, interests, or aspirations; frequent shifts in self-perception.

Some common descriptions emerge when adult children talk about their loved one with BPD: chameleon, jellyfish, the leopard who changes his spots. Depending on whom they're with and what they feel they need to portray to others, parents with BPD may frequently change their thoughts, opinions, even values. Some people with BPD can't decide which December holiday to celebrate or what faith they should follow.

"Who are you anyway, Mother?" I'd whisper to myself after I was sent to my room for some perceived wrong I committed." says Rose. "It was a ritual for me. I'd close the door, sit on my bed, and ask that question. At forty-three, I still don't know the answer; she was everchanging, like she couldn't stand to be in her own skin for too long."

"It was like Halloween every day," says Maria, the grown daughter of a borderline father. "We never knew what mask and costume he'd be wearing next week. One day he came home wearing a black leather outfit, with a brand new Harley Davidson parked on the front lawn. That was early spring. About a month later, he called my mother from his office—he's a CPA—and told her to bring us all down to the yacht club. There, he showed us the new sailboat he'd bought. This time, he was wearing what my siblings and I now jokingly refer to as his 'captain costume'—khaki twill pants, light blue oxford shirt, navy blazer with insignia and boat shoes. That he used to tell us he hated the water made the scene seem all the more surreal. We kids still remember that day in colorful detail."

The take-aways may include

◊ The person with BPD needs me so much, I'm being taken over; it's like we're one.

◊ This person isn't real.

◊ I can't hold him to what he says because tomorrow it may change.

◊ The self is fluid.

◊ We all wear masks; what we present to the world isn't necessarily related to who we are.

4. Impulsive, often reckless, self-harming behaviors in areas such as substance abuse, binge eating, overspending, promiscuous sex, reckless driving, shoplifting.

Researchers estimate that the prevalence of substance abuse among the borderline population is about 30 percent. Eating disorders show up in about 20 percent (Gunderson 2002). Those with BPD may also exhibit impulsive behavior through repeated affairs or unsafe sex. Others spend recklessly, acquiring material items in an effort to define themselves, or gamble compulsively. The impulsive behavior may look like that of a young child, who wants what she wants when she wants it and seems oblivious to potential consequences. A toddler saying, "Now! I want it now!" strikes an all-too familiar chord in someone with a borderline parent.

One young man recalls his mother's endless run of "derelict" boy-friends after her divorce from his father. "I know you're not supposed to judge someone based on looks, but these guys were scary—and it was one after the next. I was just a kid, but I doubt it was a healthy 'habit.'"

Another man recalls being taken out driving by his drunken father. "He could barely walk, let alone drive. He was reckless—speeding like a demon, doing donuts right there in the road, burning rubber all over the place. As protective as I felt toward him, I used to wish the police would catch him and lock him up for a while so he'd have to stop. He just seemed hell-bent on killing both of us."

The take-aways may include

◊ I have to care for this person.

◊ I can make them stop acting impulsively if I just. . . .

◊ If only I were a better son/daughter, she wouldn't do these things or have these problems.

◊ I have no influence (or too much influence) over another person.

5. Repeated suicide attempts or threats, or self-injuring behaviors.

BPD suicide rates are high: between 8 and 10 percent of those with the disorder take their own lives, according to the *DSM-IV* (APA 1994). Others may threaten suicide, make non-lethal attempts, or use threats as a tool to convey their desperation to others to evoke a desired response.

One adult child of a borderline parent recalls begging her father not to follow through with a divorce from her mother, convinced her mother would kill herself if he did. One night her mother had crawled into bed with her and said, "I don't know what I'll do if Daddy leaves. I'd have to put a bullet through my head. But you and your younger brother will be fine without me—Daddy and his new wife can take care of you."

The take-aways may include

◊ If the person with BPD dies, or attempts to die, it's my fault.

◊ I'm responsible for keeping him/her from getting hurt or dying.

◊ I'm bad; if I were better, my parent wouldn't need to hurt him/herself.

◊ The reactions of others are my fault (when negative) and within my control.

6. Frequent mood swings and intense emotional reactions, irritability or anxiety of changing duration—anywhere from a few hours to a few days.

Adult children often refer to the mood swings of BPD as being like "Dr. Jekyll-Mr. Hyde," switching from happy and loving to furious, fearful, or depressed within hours or less. Often, the person himself doesn't remember—or claims not to remember—what was said or done during his previous feeling state or mood. Loved ones say things like, "When I came home two hours later, he acted like nothing had happened!"

"I don't think I'll ever forget my college graduation," says Joseph, the forty-one-year-old son of a father with BPD. "My father seemed so proud, telling all his friends I'd earned my degree and that I'd landed a great job in Manhattan (which I had). He actually told me how much he admired what I'd done—a big deal since he wasn't big into praise or expressing himself. Then in the car on the way home from a post-ceremony dinner, I laughed when my brother made a joke about my aunt's lousy cooking. My father slammed on the brakes, spun around to face me, and with daggers in his eyes proceeded to ream me for forgetting my roots and thinking I was better than everyone else because I'd been the first in the family to graduate from college. He only railed for a few minutes, but he said some of the most hurtful things ever. To this day, whenever something special happens, I hesitate to enjoy it—I'm always wondering when it'll come crashing down."

The take-aways may include

◊ I never know from one hour to the next what I'm in for.

◊ I learn to notice the most subtle of cues so that I have some warning as to what's coming.

◊ I don't trust what you tell me, because days, hours, minutes later, it could—and likely will—change.

◊ It's better not to get excited or feel good about circumstances or accomplishments because my happiness may trigger a violent reaction.

◊ It's just easier not to bask in the glow of good things, because it may be quickly followed by humiliation.

7. Ongoing or frequent feelings of being hollow, empty, or fake.

People with BPD commonly report a deep sense of boredom or a profound emptiness, which is why they may turn to drugs or alcohol, become obsessed with money and possessions, or harm themselves. Lacking a strong core, a sense of self they can trust, they feel out of control and dependent upon others, forever victimized. Despite their sometimes larger than life, hard to ignore exterior, those with BPD are sometimes described by loved ones and clinicians as seeming hollow and as putting up a façade.

"My mother would go around acting like the 'Perfect Mom,' telling others about the wonderful meals she cooked, the clever parenting tricks she used to get us to behave, how she wanted nothing but the best for us," recalls another woman. "Sure, she did some of those things—on rare occasion. Generally, she was inconsistent and sabotaging, and we never knew when she'd blow up and then give us the silent treatment, lock us out of the house, or punish us for some unknown transgression. It was like she had this image of what the perfect mother should be, and she actually believed it fit her. Most of the time, though, she failed miserably and blamed us for her shortcomings. It was understood that what went on inside our house was private and not to be shared with outsiders. Anyway, most of the time she had us all so convinced that we deserved what we got that we'd be ashamed to tell anyone a thing."

The take-aways may include

- ◊ I can't rely on you; you're not really there.
- ◊ I have to keep quiet and protect you, or else...
- ◊ I'm responsible for your self-image.
- ◊ I'm responsible for making you feel whole.

8. Either underexpressed or overexpressed feelings of anger, seen in frequent displays of temper, rage, recurrent physical fights, or extreme sarcasm or withdrawal.

Rages. Many adult children know them all too well, whether the trigger is a coat hung askew in the closet, a spilled drink, a loud TV, sickness, the suggestion that the person with BPD doesn't remember something the way others do, or a request for a divorce. Whether precipitated by something seemingly trivial or serious, the storm—not uncommonly comprised of verbal assaults or physical abuse—can subside just as quickly as it rolled in. Some recipients of the rage report the need to run away—out of the house, out of the car, or to safety in a locked room—so fearful are they of the loss of control and capacity for violence in their parent with BPD.

Because of difficulties dealing with anger, those with BPD may demonstrate passive-aggressive behavior, like one woman who would initiate hair-pulling contests with her teenaged daughter. They'd pull until one or the other held a clump of hair in her hand, or the pain was too much and someone gave in, all in "fun," of course.

"I was about four years old," recalls Lizbeth, forty-six, "cowering under the kitchen table. My mother was crouched in front of me, walling me in, rubbing my face into the plate of food I supposedly asked for and then hadn't finished. She made me walk around with chunks of scrambled egg in my hair until she was ready to bathe me and wash it out. Over the years, she'd tell the story to others and say, 'That's why she's a little off now. She was abused,' and she'd laugh—cackle is more like it."

Those with BPD may go to great lengths to deflect anger in others, which can be infuriating to a loved one trying to communicate honest feelings. Parents with BPD may not accept responsibility for their behavior, nor be willing to listen to how they might have caused emotional or physical harm. If you try to point out their behavior, they may lash out with an abusive tirade or stone-cold silence, attempting to place blame on you instead ("If you hadn't done this, I wouldn't have had to beat you").

"I wasn't 'allowed' to be angry as a child," says Robert. "Whenever I raised my voice, almost always in response to some untrue accusation of manipulating my borderline mother in some way, I was banished to my room. When I protested, I was told, 'We'll discuss it when you're rational.' We never did. I'd get the silent treatment for days at a time, and then all of a sudden, like someone flipped a light switch, I was human again and would be spoken to rather than glared at. I'd write long notes, explaining that I hadn't lied or manipulated; I'd fill in the pieces she seemed to have missed. I'd leave the notes for her at night. I'd always end them by saying I was sorry she was upset and that I loved her. The next day I'd find them, sometimes unopened or crumpled in a ball, in the trash. I'd ask if she'd gotten my note. 'We'll discuss it later.' After years of this, when I was a teenager, she said to me, 'You seem very angry.' Huh, imagine that. Sixteen years of being stifled, blamed for things I hadn't done, told I was irrational by someone who wasn't exactly acting rationally, and not given a chance to speak. Imagine having three minutes on the witness stand to defend your life, except that opposing counsel gets to duct-tape your mouth shut. 'How perceptive of you,' I wanted to say. 'You're damn right, I'm angry.'"

The take-aways may include

- ◊ I shouldn't express my feelings, especially anger.

- ◊ I have to watch what I say or I might make you violently angry.

- ◊ Rage and contrition cycle so quickly, they don't seem to be related. Feelings seem random, not necessarily in response to external stimuli.

- ◊ Stifling my feelings is the safest thing to do.

9. Brief extreme periods of mistrust, paranoia, or feelings of unreality (numbness, disconnection).

Those close to someone with BPD may notice brief fogs or spells of being out of it—brief breaks with reality or psychotic episodes. When confronting someone with BPD for their inappropriate behavior, perhaps a lie or simply recalling a conversation, adult children have described a blank look. At the time, the parent may have spaced out. He or she truly may not remember.

Adult children may also recall many accusations and their parents' readiness to blame and to assume ill intent on the part of others.

Dave, twenty-nine, says, "If a lasagna wasn't fully baked when the oven timer went off, someone else must have deliberately turned the temperature down. If I didn't call her at work at 3:30 to say I was home from school, I must have had friends over and was partying. If she couldn't find her favorite pen (because she left it somewhere and forgot), one of the kids stole it. The accusations never stopped. But the scary thing is, she really believed the little scenarios she cooked up, regardless of how far from the truth they were."

The take-aways may include

- ◊ I remember reality differently than you do. Since you seem so sure of your recollection (and you're the adult), I must be wrong.

- ◊ I misinterpreted the event.

- ◊ I can't trust my own judgment.

- ◊ I just don't get people.

- ◊ If I'm perfect, if I do everything just right, I won't be subject to false accusations.

◆ I have to always prove my case and be at the ready to defend my actions. My choices, simply because they're what I decided (based on my needs and preferences), aren't valid or acceptable.

A Fairy-Tale Model

In her book, *Understanding the Borderline Mother*, author Christine Ann Lawson (2000) uses fairy-tale personalities—the waif, the queen, the hermit, the witch—to describe borderline traits. While these categories can help you identify the disorder and its various aspects and help you understand your childhood experience, people with BPD or its traits may at times exhibit behavior that overlaps categories. As you read the following brief descriptions based on Lawson's work, which applies to men and women alike, keep in mind that your parent may show characteristics of more than one type, and different people within your family may have been exposed to different traits.

The Waif

The waif feels like a helpless victim. She (or he) may appear social but never really engage with others on a deeper level. She may be "inappropriately open" and then reject those with whom she's just shared; "fish for compliments" and then deny them; complain and then wave away suggestions and offers of help. The waif feels hopeless and anticipates negativity, even before she has any evidence that it might be in store.

Characteristics of a waif parent include permissiveness, alternately spoiling and neglecting children, and using fantasies of a fairy tale life to distract from reality. The waif is more likely to cry than rage, and to suffer from anxiety and depression.

Messages from a waif parent may include: Life is so hard; nobody loves me; I have it a lot worse than you/others.

The Queen

The queen feels empty yet entitled. She yearns for material wealth, beauty, attention and loyalty. Queen parents may compete with a child for attention, feel jealous of their child's achievements or attributes and act in selfish and domineering ways. When others comment on or challenge the queen's beliefs or behavior, she may paint them as the enemy.

Characteristics of a queen parent include expecting his or her children to see things the same way and to be loyal; dramatic or histrionic behavior; and a tendency toward exaggeration. The queen has a hard time respecting others' boundaries and preferences. Despite her needs, she may come across as quite strong and independent.

Messages children of queen parents may receive include: You must love me; I resent you when you need something from me.

The Hermit

The hermit feels fear; he's always on alert against potential danger. He may seem paranoid at times, perceiving threats where others don't. Phobias or superstitions may interfere with daily living. Benign or even helpful comments from others may be interpreted as a threat or attack. Hermits can be excessively self-protecting, possessive, and domineering. They may seem hypersensitive and feel violated when someone touches or borrows something that belongs to them. When angry, they may fly into a rage or give the "silent treatment."

Messages from a hermit parent include: The world is a scary, dangerous place; They won't stop until they get me.

The Witch

Witches feel white-hot rage. Few borderline parents consistently exhibit witch-like behavior. Rather, the witch seems to emerge from the waif, queen, or hermit when triggered by perceived rejection or her own self-hatred. Witches may use shame and embarrassment of their children as parenting tools.

Witch parents can be domineering and vindictive; they may seem to repeatedly be at the center of conflict when it arises. They may have a hard time respecting others' boundaries and may ruin a child's cherished possessions, give away or euthanize a child's pets, or withhold affection or care. They may be physically abusive as well.

Witch parents may send the following messages: Boy, will you regret that; You asked for it.

Defying Classification

Adult children share a host of common experiences which we will examine further in chapter 2. One of the most difficult things can be the lack of validation of your childhood pain. People with BPD don't always appear "crazy." Many are quite high-functioning, appearing perfectly healthy to the outside world. This can make children doubt their own judgment, and it can undermine their sense of self-worth. Children see Mom or Dad acting in normal ways with some people and then cruelly at home, and they come to believe they're the cause of their parent's negative and/or inconsistent behavior.

Acting Out Versus Acting In

In *Stop Walking on Eggshells: Taking Your Life Back When Someone You Care About Has Borderline Personality Disorder*, Kreger and Mason (1998) identify two groups: those with BPD that *act in* and those that *act out*.

Those that act out tend to function well in public; they are doctors and managers, lawyers and parents, best friends and board members; they're politicians and teachers. They are often fun to be around. They may be ambitious, successful professionally, the life of the party, sociable, and great storytellers. They may have a knack for putting others at ease. Once out of the public eye, however, they direct their negative emotion at others—usually family members—pointing an accusatory finger, making impossible demands, and inflicting verbal, emotional, and sometimes physical abuse on loved ones. (Some adult children recall being told as adolescents that they were ugly, unpopular, and wouldn't amount to anything, for example.) From outward appearances, the person with BPD may seem the model of competence and normalcy. Some do well except under stress or in particular areas of their lives—for example, the person who is an award-winning professional, brilliant and well-respected, but who unravels at home with her kids and husband when the household chores aren't done properly and in a timely manner. Their personal lives and intimate relationships may be intensely chaotic, making it all the more difficult for family members, particularly children, to ask for help—or even to realize something isn't normal.

Others with BPD act in, tending instead to turn negative emotion inward, resulting in self-destructive behaviors such as cutting, self-mutilation, abusing alcohol or drugs, feeling intensely guilty for circumstances and events beyond their control, setting unreasonably high standards for themselves, or attempting suicide. They tend to be heavy utilizers of the mental health, and health care systems, and may have difficulty keeping a permanent job. (BPD comprises about 10 percent of the outpatient mental health patient population and 15 to 20 percent of the inpatient population (APA 2001).)

It's important to note that the acting-in and acting-out or high- and low-functioning labels are not mutually exclusive. Those with the disorder may show signs of both. One woman, now "divorced" from her borderline mother after years of suicide threats and attempts, explains how her mother had trouble holding down jobs and had an addiction to prescription medications, but was popular among her circle of friends. "She was such a sweet person to others; she'd give you the shirt off her back."

BPD exists along a spectrum, running the gamut from mild to severe as well as occurring with other psychiatric disturbances. Some adult children may recall superficially normal childhoods, with all the trappings of material wealth and success but with strange or erratic behavior and subtle but insidious emotional abuse at home. Others recall a parent who had trouble getting out of bed in the morning, rarely cleaned the house or bought groceries, who may have been hospitalized for repeated suicide attempts or severe addiction. There's only one constant with BPD, and that's inconsistency.

Picking Up the Signals

Children learn from their parents. Almost as soon as you made your debut in the world, you took cues from your parents as to what this place would be like and your role within it. If your primary teachers were working from a confusing lesson plan, you may have absorbed some unhelpful, unhealthy messages as you developed.

The messages children may receive from parents with BPD include

◊ I'm a victim; you hurt me and/or it's your responsibility to take care of me.

◊ I have no control; I'm not to be held accountable for what I say or do. I may not even accurately remember what transpired.

◊ My needs come first. When I do something for you, it's possible I'm doing it to satisfy some need I have (giving you a gift makes me feel like I'm being a good parent; it's less about you than about me).

◊ No one understands me. No one could possibly understand how hard I have it, how difficult my life is, what I'm going through.

◊ I am entitled; (alternately) I am worthless, in which case it's your responsibility to bolster my sense of self. I rely on you—better not let me down.

◊ My perspective is right; the rest of the world is wrong. But nobody listens to me.

STOP AND THINK: Record Your Messages

Are there other messages you heard from your parent? Record them in your journal, and include what your parent said or did that conveyed the message.

STOP AND THINK: The Lessons Are Clear

As you read through the following list, ask yourself if you learned any of the following lessons as a child and if they still affect you now. Don't judge yourself ("I shouldn't have felt that way"). Just see if anything resonates.

- You can't trust others, even those that are close to you because your confidence is often—and randomly—betrayed.

- You're damned if you do, and damned if you don't; you just can't do *anything* right.

- It's unsafe to express your true feelings, because they will be mocked, denigrated, or ignored.

- You can't trust yourself, since your perceptions are usually corrected.

- People manipulate; gifts come with strings attached.

- Life holds little physical affection—few hugs or pats on the head.

- You are undeserving of love and affection, compliments, or material items.

- You are guilty of being a burden, for the sacrifices your parent made for you, for being angry, for disagreeing, for having your own needs, for being a child, for being your own person.

- It's risky to assert yourself; others' needs, desires, and opinions come first.

Are there other lessons you learned?

It's a long list, and one that's likely painful to read through as you identify aspects within yourself today that you may not be especially proud of or happy with. And you might simultaneously be sighing with relief as you read—from the recognition that you weren't, and aren't, alone; that a private, personal experience is indeed shared by others. Take a deep breath and rest assured that understanding the disorder and its fallout is the first step toward recognizing your authentic self and building a positive and healthy future.

CHAPTER 2

All Grown Up

In this chapter, we'll discuss some of the conditions children with a parent with BPD may live with and the common effects on adult children. We'll also talk about positive childhood experiences you may have had, the effect of adult role models, and the development of inner resilience and resources.

Keep in mind that the purpose of this book is not to blame a parent with BPD or its traits but to identify patterns that affect your life today. With a better understanding of how they may have developed, envisioning and working toward change will come more readily.

What You Experienced

You may recognize some of the conditions and experiences described below, including chaos, abuse and neglect, boundary violations, and invalidation, or you may have had a somewhat different or opposing experience. Use your own circumstances to consider the thoughts, beliefs, feelings, and behaviors you may have learned growing up and how they shaped who you are today.

Chaos

Since they don't have a strong sense of identity, people with BPD may simultaneously fear abandonment and engulfment, hence the *I Hate You-Don't Leave Me* title of a seminal book on the disorder (Kreisman and

Straus 1991). In the interviews we conducted, adult children tell of grow-ing up in a confusing and unpredictable world. They rarely knew what to expect—whether they'd be praised or berated, hugged or brushed off, smothered or neglected. Some wondered from hour to hour what they should be thinking or doing to gain their parent's approval. One day the parent might be having a "lucid moment," which several adult children called the period of time where their parent seemed to be relating to oth-ers in a healthy way, actually present rather than dissociating, denying, or projecting. During these times, the parent might encourage the child to develop his or her self but then later on be outright angry that the child did just that. Or the discouragement might be more subtle, as in sabotage or silent treatment for no apparent reason.

Mary, now in her fifties, recalls her mother sometimes encouraging her to be more outgoing. "Why don't you have any friends?" her mother would ask cruelly. "You need to make more of an effort." At about fifteen or sixteen years old, she got to know a small group of girls at her high school. Whenever she'd spend the night at one of their homes, her mother would accuse her of lying, of saying she was sleeping over so that she and "those sluts you've been spending so much time with" could stay out late with boys. Her mother also refused to give her rides to her girlfriends' houses or to pick her up from places they'd go. "Since they like you so much, let them chauffeur you around."

Mary still can't reconcile her mother's contradictory behavior: "You're damned if you do, and damned if you don't. I wish she'd kept her mouth shut about the whole issue of friends; she really didn't want me to have them; she saw them as a threat to my relationship with her, even though at times she knew a 'good mother' should encourage me. But criti-cizing me and then making those relationships nearly impossible was cruel. I know about BPD on an intellectual level, but as her daughter, thirty-something years later, I still don't understand."

People with BPD traits appear to move from one crises to the next. They may be disorganized; their living quarters may be sloppy, even dirty, or the extreme opposite. Adult children often recall that crises were common, and when life didn't provide one naturally, they could count on their parent to create or seek one out, whether picking a fight in order to rage, entering into an unhealthy relationship, or abandoning an existing partner (but then very likely seeking a quick reconciliation).

Because of BPD's cognitive distortions, or perceiving a reality altered by their own idealizations and projections, parents with BPD see themselves differently than they actually are. They may see themselves as caring and nur-turing when they have been indifferent or cruel; they may see themselves as the perfect parent, homemaker, or provider; they may not have an inkling as to how their actual behavior is affecting those around them—or how confusing and chaotic those distortions are for their children.

The Effects: Escape from Reality

As a result of the unpredictability, children of parents with BPD often find a physical or psychic place to retreat—their bedroom, a closet, or rich imaginary worlds they create. Adult children report missing chunks of memory; they look back and wonder what they did with their time. They may (and may continue to) dissociate, or zone out, for periods of time ranging from a few seconds to even hours.

One woman raised by a mother with BPD, who alternated between being "all loving" and "a yelling, screaming, bitter, angry, rageful person—like someone carrying a hand grenade; you never knew when she was about to pull the pin," says her dissociation is a repercussion of growing up in constant fear of her mother's explosions. "I froze my emotions; I didn't allow myself to feel. My major way of coping was saying, 'This just isn't where I am.' I did it to such an extent that I missed a lot of what happened in school. A large part of my childhood is just blank."

Today, she is more mindful of where she is and what she's doing, not living as much in her head as she used to. Yet her dissociating is a continual source of contention between her and her husband, who gets frustrated that she often misplaces items and forgets to do things around the house, that despite her physical proximity, she's not always present.

Adult children may get lost in fantasies and/or daydreams, having the tendency to idealize situations and people. They may see a fairy-tale, whitewashed version of reality rather than what's actually in front of them. In some cases, they see what they'd wished their home and family relationships would have been like when they were children. Or they may see what their parent with BPD idealized and projected ("This is the kind of family you *should* have . . ."). As adults, this idealization may be manifest in unrealistic demands on others, including friends, sons and daughters, and partners, and unrealistic expectations of relationships. They expect perfection and as a result are ultimately disappointed since nothing and no one is perfect.

Abuse and Neglect

Some adult children speak of living with emotional cruelty, severe physical violence, and/or neglect. Roslyn, fifty-two, describes herself as a "feral child," improperly fed, denied medical care, clothed with one out-fit—worn until it was in tatters—for her four years of high school, raged at, and beaten at random. Others recall severe beratings seemingly trig-gered by something as inconsequential as not setting the table properly, oversleeping, or vomiting. They experienced outright hatred or resent-ment, and even as children wondered why their parents ever had them.

Given that substance abuse and other self-harming and impulsive behaviors occur frrequently in BPD, drinking, doing drugs, sexual addic-tions, stealing, or gambling may have taken precedence over parenting responsibilities. Evelyn, forty-one, remembers making a suicide attempt when she was a teenager. She was lying on the floor in her room, groggy from the pills she'd taken, when her mother rushed in, furious that her Valium was missing.

Furthermore, given the deep fears of abandonment and lack of a well-defined sense of self, parents with BPD are often attracted to emo-tionally immature mates. Some adult children describe a second parent (or stepparent) who was extremely codependent and didn't often stand up to the person with BPD. Others describe a parent who was extremely narcis-sistic, or otherwise unavailable. Children of these couples are in effect emotionally abandoned by not one but two parents who are limited by their own emotional needs.

The Effects: Post-Traumatic Stress and Long-Term Illness

As a result of living with verbal, emotional, physical or sexual abuse, adult children may suffer from post-traumatic stress disorder (PTSD) even years after leaving their family of origin.

Moira, a thirty-three-year-old woman, now married and an archi-tect, was raised by a mother with BPD and a father who wasn't present very much. When he was, he often acquiesced to her demands and deferred to her on issues relating to their three children. Moira's therapist diagnosed her with PTSD when Moira was in her late twenties. She'd been having troubling nightmares about her family where she'd wake up screaming, usually at her mother. Though she hadn't lived at home since she was eighteen, she says she was still feeling the rage that had been pent up, but stifled by her mother, for so many years. In addition to having nightmares, Moira felt numb, completely out of touch with her emotions, and she was hyperaroused, or constantly watching for the tiniest clues and signals in others that would indicate a pending "attack"—physical, mental, or emotional. Moira says she was unable to trust anyone then, even the man who is now her husband; she startled easily and would jump at sudden noises or movements. "Even though I wasn't ever physically abused as a child, as an adult, I was tense almost all the time. Rick would come up behind me to hug or kiss me, and I'd stiffen or jump. I knew he was trying to be affectionate, but I hated it. Any kind of physical touch was difficult. Forget about our sex life."

Some adult children who lived with physical and/or emotional abuse from a parent also report that the abuse manifests in physical illnesses, including irritable bowel syndrome (IBS), fibromyalgia, asthma, migraines, and other autoimmune and stress-related disorders.

Boundary Violations

Those with BPD have a hard time negotiating the boundaries between themselves and others. Each time a child knowingly or unknowingly asserts him- or herself or calls attention to the boundary between self and parent, it may trigger feelings of rejection and abandonment in someone with BPD.

Boundary violations include any type of physical or sexual abuse; any infringement upon personal space, such as walking into the bathroom or bedroom without knocking; and not respecting a child's right to privacy or ownership (for example, reading a child's diary or giving away the child's possessions without asking). Boundaries defining a child's emotional space may be violated as well when a parent asks detailed personal questions or demands that children share information they haven't volunteered.

Catherine, twenty-three, recalled her mother treating her more like a friend than a daughter, sharing inappropriate details of her sex life and an extra-marital affair, which she expected Catherine to keep secret from her father.

Michael, thirty-four, remembers his mother asking him "way too many" questions about his father and his father's new wife whenever he got home from a visit with them. When he was older, she asked too many questions when he'd come home from a date.

Enmeshment

Because the parent has such a blurred sense of self in relation to others, enmeshment, or emotional entanglement, is common. Borderline parents may treat their children as an extension of themselves, almost like one of their limbs, expecting them to wear the same style clothes, hold the same opinions, or to side with them in disagreements with a spouse or other family members.

The parent may be jealous of the child's relationships with the other parent, grandparents, brothers and sisters, friends, even pets. Nancy, twenty-two, recalls her mother telling her, "Go ahead, go up to your room and cry to that mangy dog of yours." Kim, thirty-two, recalls the repeated accusation against her and her sister: "You're ganging up on me." For someone with BPD, life is a zero-sum game, particularly when it comes to love—it seems like there's not enough to go around. The thought process appears to be, "If you love your father, you must not love me," or, "If you want to spend time with someone else, you're abandoning me. If you have a relationship with someone else, you're disloyal to me."

Lisa, the thirty-four-year-old daughter of a woman with BPD, recalls the difficulty she had trying to separate from her mother. "With all her wacky schemes, Mother was like a square peg trying to fit in a round hole. For my entire life, she tried to put me in the round hole with her. I wanted to say, 'But I'm not a square peg!' My main goal was to make sure she was happy. And I was her; there was no separation." When Lisa's mother divorced her father and then her stepfather, she would say, "We divorced," rather than, "I divorced," Lisa recalls. That was one of numerous examples. "It robbed me of my self-esteem, my identity. I existed for her. Whenever I tried to exist for myself, she blew up at me."

Macy, thirty-seven, recalls the look of surprise on her father's face when as a teenager she burst into tears at her grandmother's funeral. He seemed dumbfounded that she was grieving, that she had and was expressing her own emotions at a moment when he was composed.

The Effects: Walking on Eggshells

Children learn to tiptoe around, to limit the activities that seem to trigger a parent's upset, and to minimize contact with others so that the parent isn't threatened by those relationships. Some children may rebel, spending long periods of time out of the house, engaging in promiscuous or other impulsive behaviors.

From the enmeshment they experienced as children and often into adulthood, sons and daughters may feel that they can't live life independently while maintaining a relationship with their parent. They report ongoing blowups and meltdowns when the everyday things they do trigger parents' fears and insecurities. If adult children get married, make a commitment to a partner, or have children, for instance, they fear—or based on their experience, they know—their parent will interfere in some way.

Nita, fifty, puts it in strikingly simple terms: "Sometimes the guilt makes me feel like a monster, but I'll admit there are times I've wished for [my mother's] death. It's the only way I think I'll ever feel truly free."

Because of the boundary violations they may have experienced while growing up, adult children report difficulty navigating boundaries and setting appropriate limits with others.

Invalidation

Children of parents with BPD may experience implicit or explicit invalidation. Their feelings got downplayed or ignored, or they are taught that their perceptions are wrong. Some adults recall being interrupted when they tried to express their feelings or repeatedly asked things such as, "Well, what did *you* do to make this happen?" implying that whatever happened was their fault. They may recall being asked a question and, when they replied, having their parent rage at them for an apparently wrong answer.

Adult children remember other common responses when they disclosed information or tried to share their feelings: "You're making it out to be worse than it really is," "You just don't understand," "You don't know what it's like," "You don't appreciate...," "Girls/boys your age don't feel [sad, scared, angry, etc.]."

The Effects: Second-Guessing

Children, and later, adults, learn to distrust their own judgment. They second-guess their decisions and wonder if they've neglected to think of something. Since they were repeatedly told they were misinterpreting things, they may have difficulty identifying their own feelings. They may feel tremendously guilty for feeling their own emotions, thinking their own thoughts and doing what they want to do since, from a young age, they may have been admonished for not considering their parent's needs before their own.

Role Reversals

Children of parents with BPD are often parentified; that is, they learn to act as caretaker, perhaps for their siblings or for their parent(s). Many adult children have trouble recalling times when they just felt like fun-loving, silly kids. Some remember the chore lists they were given as children—not a few "to do" items like making their bed, cleaning their room, taking out trash, or other age-appropriate tasks, but major projects that included cleaning basements, preparing family meals, landscaping, and doing the family laundry. They may have been expected to get jobs at a young age or buy their own clothes with the money rattling around in their piggy banks.

Though she was scared of dogs from the time she was bitten as a five-years-old, Vivian, thirty, reports having been made to clean up the yard daily after the family dog—the same one that bit her.

Though he often babysat and cleaned, Juan, twenty-eight, recalls being commanded one day to clean the house and put up some decorations for company, which turned out to be visiting for his own "surprise" tenth birthday party.

With parents who attempted suicide or had substance abuse issues, adult children recall literally being responsible for their parent's life, hiding pill bottles, calling paramedics, or making sure drunken adults found their way to a couch or bed without getting hurt.

Ed, forty-three, remembers his mother asking him from the time he was about eight years old to call her boss whenever she was too hung over to get herself to work.

The Effects: Everyone Else Comes First

Rather than act like kids, parentified children learn to take responsibility for themselves and others early on. They tend to fade into the woodwork and let others take center stage. This extends into adulthood—adult children may put others' needs before their own. They may have difficulty accepting care and attention. It's hard for them to feel happy and content. They may seem old before their time or like an old soul (and probably were that way as children too). They may easily assume the role of fixer and nurturer. They're the ones friends lean on, the ones to whom people tell their problems. Helping others gives them a sense of purpose and worth.

Looks Are *Everything*

With a fragile and shifting sense of self in a borderline parent, material items and keeping up with the Joneses are often a part of many adult children's early experience.

Ilana reports that her mother bought a brand-new expensive car every year on a meager salary, while the living room furniture was in dire need of replacement. Her mother continued to rack up tremendous debt, but having that symbol of status was important to her.

Roberto's father continually complained about not earning enough money to pay his bills every month, yet he'd buy the latest, greatest electronic equipment that seemed out of scale in the family's modest home.

Borderline parents with an insecure sense of self may use jewelry, clothes, and other trappings as proof of their attainment of the idealized happy family, regardless of their means. Rather than unconditional love, nurturance, and open communication, the emphasis may have been on how things appeared to outsiders. Thus the need for expensive cars, respectable jobs, obedient children, well-groomed pets, a carefully landscaped yard.

The Effects: Materialism, Self-Denial

Adult children may have learned to focus on appearances too and to judge others by their status, class background, possessions, where they went to college, what car they drive, who they know. They may hold themselves to the same high material standards as well, not feeling good about themselves unless they have the newest, the biggest, the most expensive. Conversely, they may use material possessions to punish themselves, denying themselves new or good quality items because they don't feel deserving.

Carolyn says it wasn't until her fortieth birthday last year when her husband gave her gift certificates to a day spa and an upscale department store that she was able to spend on herself without feeling guilty. "Before then, I felt just fine wearing whatever was in my closet and shopping at second-hand stores. Not that there's anything wrong with that, but I realized that buying something nice for myself or having a massage once in a while is okay. I never felt like I deserved that kind of treatment before."

Keen Perception

Those with BPD may exhibit a hypersensitivity and reactivity to external stimuli, including others' facial expressions, body language, and tone of voice. Adult children report being told they smelled bad or had bad breath, that they need to brush their teeth, shower more often, try a new brand of anti-perspirant or stop eating garlic.

This sensitivity to their surroundings may related to the anxiety that many with BPD feel. They're often fearful of many things— crowds, open spaces, being left alone even for a short time, being hurt or made to look foolish, losing a job, driving. They may commonly suspect or accuse others of conspiring against them. "You're manipulating me" or "you don't want me to be happy" is not an uncommon complaint. Life for the parent with BPD may appear to be an obstacle course of booby traps maliciously set by those around them, against which they must always be on guard.

The Effects: Self-Consciousness, Perfectionism

Adult children may have learned to be shy and self-conscious about their physical appearance, behavior, and emotions. They may tend toward perfectionism since no matter what they did, it was never quite enough. And they may feel guilty for their thoughts and feelings.

Transference

Parents with BPD may project, or transfer feelings onto children (or others) to avoid accepting them as his or her own. Let's say someone with BPD clips coupons and presents them to the cashier at the grocery store. She perceives a look of annoyance or pity on the part of another shopper, a complete stranger, in the check-out line. Whether or not the other shopper was annoyed or feeling sorry for her, she feels embarrassed and guilty for holding up the line. When she gets home, she watches as her daughter does the laundry. "Use more soap," orders the mother. "Why are you so stingy?" What's really going through her subconscious mind is, "I feel stingy, but it's easier for me to believe it's you than to accept those feelings about myself."

A father with BPD continually told his teenage son, Bo, he'd make a lousy father one day and that he should stay a bachelor all his life. It wasn't until Bo was in his mid-thirties, had fallen in love, and planned to marry that he and his wife-to-be discussed plans for a family. At first he said he never wanted children, but she pointed out to him that he was good with kids and seemed to enjoy them. He cherished the time he spent with his nieces and nephews; he coached soccer, and he assisted with the youth group at his church. The more he thought about it, he realized he'd always liked being around kids, but it was the tape from his father that looped in his head. Bo came to realize, "It was my father who wasn't meant for this; he's the one who never should have had kids."

The Effects: Anger, Weak Sense of Self

Adult children who served as the screen for their parents' projections may feel intense anger at their parent for continually overriding their thoughts and beliefs. They may lack a well-defined sense of self, because it's hard to know who you really are when someone is superimposing their views onto you, telling you it's really what *you* believe or want.

What We Know

Numerous studies have been conducted to ascertain the impact of having an alcoholic, depressed, or generally mentally ill parent, but very few studies have focused on BPD specifically. The one study we located, published in the *Canadian Journal of Psychiatry* in 1996, was conducted with twenty-one children of mothers with BPD and twenty-three children of nonborderline mothers. It found that the former group had more psychiatric diagnoses, more impulse control disorders, and a higher risk of BPD themselves (Weiss et. al. 1996).

Certainly many of the effects of family-of-origin dysfunction on adult children are thought by researchers to be similar (Rubio-Stipec et al. 1991). These effects include

- ◊ increased risk of depression

- ◊ suicide attempts

- ◊ poor self-esteem

- ◊ social anxiety

- ◊ issues related to intimacy.

Just as singing children all fall down in the game "Ring around the Rosie," adult children feel like they too fell down, like they failed as children and are flawed or "defective," a word used by several people in interviews. The way they felt as children continues into adulthood.

Others talk of a fundamental sense of shame and dogged perfectionism, regardless of their accomplishments or relationships. Maryanne's eyes welled up during an interview as she wondered if she'd ever be able to have a truly emotionally intimate relationship, or even feel entitled to "breathing room on the planet."

Patterns of Attachment

The lasting effects on children raised by a parent with BPD can be related to what psychiatrist John Bowlby (1969) and others have referred to as *insecure attachment patterns,* formed before children are even able to speak or comprehend language, making the consequences all the more difficult to articulate later in life. Patterns of attachment to parents or caretakers continue to develop through late adolescence, affecting lifelong relationships.

When children are raised by families responsive to their need for affection, they develop confidence in their ability to form relationships with others; they learn that they deserve comfort and kindness, that others are there to support them. They learn trust; they learn how to ask for help in times of need; and they learn to articulate their desire for and to seek affection. They possess a sense of optimism about difficult situations.

Insecure Attachment

Insecure attachments are typical of children raised by parents who are inconsistent or abusive, emotionally preoccupied by their own needs and insecurities. Children have little confidence in an available safety net, and therefore they deny their need for support and care from others. They've parented themselves, and often their siblings, from early on, and they learn not to get close to or trust others.

Insecure parental attachment patterns lead to children second-guessing themselves, wondering whether it's safe to assert themselves, make a particular choice, treat themselves in a positive way, and/or reach out to others. As adults, the inconsistency and insecurity experienced in parental relationships gets overlaid onto adult relationships with relatives, coworkers, friends, and intimate partners, rendering adult children distrustful of others' motives, on guard against hidden agendas and unsure of their own identities, judgment, and their worthiness of being unconditionally accepted and loved.

Blind Acceptance

Much of the adult child's second-guessing may have become so ingrained that she may not consciously realize she's engaging in it. Even when called to her attention, she may not readily identify her childhood experience as a possible reason why. For most people, their family of origin is the only reality they've known, so it seems perfectly normal to them, it's the standard by which they measure other relationships and interactions. And even if they realize it wasn't completely "normal," or that they weren't happy as children—or adults—they may not have much concept of how things could have been different.

The Ideal Relationship

Children want—need—to believe that their parents will provide protection. The alternative—that a parent is incapable of taking care of them—is unthinkable to a child. Children need to believe that what a parent says is logical, honest, and for their own good. Many adult children say they felt very close to their parent with BPD and that they had a healthy relationship. Some recall stretches of "good years" and now, looking back, realize they'd idealized their relationship.

That's not to say the good years didn't happen. Perhaps they were the result of the child, even the adult child, not setting boundaries with the parent so the parent didn't feel threatened or rejected. The idealized relationship may also be the result of what John Bradshaw refers to as a trance-like state in his book *Creating Love:* "What we grow up with is what we come to view as normal. Our childhood is like the air we breathe—we take it for granted" (1992, p. 24).

Often people don't even realize they can question their family relationships or the role they played within the familial structure. Bradshaw explains how, as a social system, all families need the structure that roles provide. In functional families, roles are flexible; they shift in understandable and somewhat predictable ways according to circumstances, external demands, and family members' needs. In dysfunctional families, roles tend to be rigid and unpredictable. Still, they often go unchallenged or unexamined.

Six Seeds to Grow a Healthy Child

There's no question that raising a child is an immensely difficult, yet rewarding, undertaking. No parent is perfect; all run short of patience at times, react before thinking, and on occasion wish in hindsight they could have handled a particular situation differently. In healthy families, these moments are relatively few and far between, and when they occur, parents are able to address and discuss them, even apologize to their children for them. What was a negative event can be used as a mechanism to model positive family dynamics for children.

For parents with traits of BPD, however, it's a challenge to consistently sow these seeds in offspring. They likely didn't receive them or have them modeled by their own parents when they were children, so they didn't have an appropriate, healthy point of reference. And with a fragile sense of self, they may not have been able to ask for help or accept their own shortcomings.

Without minimizing the challenges of parenting, the fundamentals of raising a healthy, confident, well-adjusted child are in fact quite straightforward. Children need support, respect and acceptance, voice, unconditional love and affection, consistency, and security.

Support

Children need to know a parent or caretaker is behind them, cheering them on emotionally and believing in their ability to succeed. Children should not be expected to provide similar or reciprocal support to parents, or to be treated as an equal, an adult, or their parent's closest ally or friend.

Respect and Acceptance

Children need to know that they have intrinsic worth, that they have the right to occupy physical, mental, and emotional space in the universe and that they can expect that space to be safe, acknowledged, and not tread upon.

Voice

Children need a sense of agency, of autonomy that instills confidence that they'll be heard and therefore that they have some level of control over their environment. Parents who foster agency, voice, in children value their opinions and needs and are able to demonstrate empathy with children's feelings. They validate; they enter the child's world, rather than expecting the child to enter theirs (Grossman, 2003).

Unconditional Love and Affection

Children need to know they're loved and will be cared for regardless of who they are, what they do, how they behave, dress, what their physical appearance and mental abilities are, or how much others like or love them. They also need affection, including being hugged and held and told they're loved.

Consistency

One of the most important seeds for a healthy child is consistency. Children who are parented with consistency learn confidence and security; they feel safe in knowing that there is some order in their world, that commitments are kept and rules followed. What a parent permits on Monday a child shouldn't then be reprimanded for on Tuesday or Thursday or Sunday, or if Mother is tired or in a bad mood, for example.

Security

Children need to feel safe and secure that they will be provided for in terms of food, clothing, shelter, emotional support, and love. Children develop their sense of security as a result of consistency.

STOP AND THINK: Six Seeds

Think of two or three incidents where your parent provided any one of the six seeds (support, respect and acceptance, voice, security, unconditional love and affection, consistency). Write them down, including the circumstances, the emotions you felt, and what you took away or gleaned about yourself.

Now think of two or three incidents where any one of these six seeds was withheld or not provided by your parent. This could be a time when you were reprimanded for something and the punishment was out of proportion with the affront; you confided in your parent and your feelings were ignored; you were told to do one thing and then soon after told to do something else, neither of which was "right"; or you were humiliated or abused. Write them down, including the circumstances, the emotions you felt, and how you explained the incident to yourself afterward. What did you take away from the experience?

How do you think all of these events and others like them affected your development in terms of your ability to feel safe, independent, valued, lovable? How did these events affect your sense of self?

How to Bounce Back

Recalling a difficult past and examining how it affected your development and your life today can be painful. Moving forward may seem overwhelming at times, but humans are amazingly resilient creatures. It's important to give yourself credit for the strength and other qualities you possess that allowed you to survive and accomplish all that you have, thus far.

In simple terms, resilience is the ability to overcome adversity. Many factors foster resilience, including social intelligence (the ability to interact with others), likeability, adaptability, mood stability, healthy supporters other than parents, curiosity, and physical health.

STOP AND THINK: Resiliency Builders

Check the characteristics you relied upon most often as a child coping with a borderline parent. In your journal, write about how you used them then, and how you use them now.

_____ Adaptable
You adjust to new, changing, or difficult situations with relative ease.

_____ Confident
You feel a sense of competence in at least some of the important areas of your life; you possess a sense of self-respect.

_____ Curious
You have an innate inquisitiveness and interest in the world around you.

_____ Engaged
You have the ability to connect with others, to give and accept support.

_____ Humorous
You're able to find humor in situations.

_____ Intuitive
You have good hunches when it comes to understanding others and how they behave.

_____ Inventive
You have the ability to see things in different ways; to come up with alternatives to problems; and to express yourself through creative endeavors.

_____ Optimistic
You possess a sense of hope and a solid belief that the future will be fine, or better.

_____ Persistent
You're tenacious and have the ability to work at something that's important to you.

_____ Self-directed
When something truly needs to be done, you're able to recognize it on your own and muster the inner resources to do it.

_____ Spiritual
You believe in some force larger than yourself and your own (and others') human abilities.

The Importance of Role Models

Mentors and role models can play a large role in helping children develop coping skills and resiliency by modeling healthy behavior, providing insight into a parent's emotional challenges or simply removing a child periodically from a dysfunctional home. Consider the following examples.

Elisabeth, a forty-two-year-old accountant raised by a mother with BPD, recalls going to visit a family friend most days after school. She'd watch TV with the friend, run errands, help her take care of her three small children, and simply observe as the friend cooked dinner. Not only was it a respite from her own tense, often chaotic home, says Elisabeth, but "I saw another way for parents to interact with their children. I couldn't have articulated the differences then, but I knew it _felt_ better. I also learned that people could enjoy my company. I always seemed to be a lot of trouble for my mother."

Rick, a twenty-seven-year-old medical resident raised by a borderline stepfather, recalls the summers he spent with his paternal grandmother from the time he was eight until the year he turned thirteen, when she became too frail to take care of him. "I used to get this sinking feeling in my stomach when my parents came to pick me up at the end of August and the whole way home in the car. They used to tell me to open the window, thinking I was carsick. I wasn't. I just didn't want to go back." Rick and his grandmother would go for walks and pick fruit. He helped her with canning, and he'd groom her two big dogs. He felt valued, but most of all he recalls the sense of peace that pervaded his grandmother's house. "It was so different from home. There were no sudden rages to worry about, no doors slamming or cruel accusations followed by days of silence and cold stares. Looking back now, it's no surprise I felt physically ill."

Mariel, nineteen and a student with a mother with BPD, spent weekends with her aunt starting when she was about twelve. "It might sound silly, but among other things, I learned how to fold laundry, towels, from her. Her house was neat. At home, things were disorganized and messy; towels were stuffed in closets. I also learned how to organize. I'd watch my aunt sort her mail, pay bills, balance her checkbook, and use a planner to track her business appointments. Seeing her do chores methodically and think ahead to the coming week helped me to know there was a way to get through the fog I felt like I was in a lot of the time. I'm not sure I would have made it through high school without learning those things from her."

STOP AND THINK: Positive Influences

Take a few minutes to reflect on your childhood and the adults who served as positive, stable forces, perhaps an aunt or uncle, teacher, grandparent, family friend, or the parent of a schoolmate. Who were those influential people in your life?

How did you feel when you were around them? What did you learn from them?

How did what you learned or observed help you better deal with your situation at home and/or your parent with BPD, even though you might not have known about BPD then? Did these other adults validate your experience at home, for example, telling you that your mother/father didn't always do the right thing or that your parent's behavior wasn't a reflection of you? What did that validation mean to you then? What does it mean to you now?

Commend yourself for your resilience. You obviously possessed talent, intuition, and knowledge that got you to where you are today. It's easy to criticize yourself for your perceived deficiencies and weaknesses, but it's important as well to recognize your strengths and your ability to overcome challenging circumstances.

CHAPTER 3

Grieving a Lost Childhood

Growing up, you may have suspected that something was wrong, that your family seemed different or unhealthy, but you may not have known what specifically was the cause. You may have seen isolated symptoms and traits of BPD but lacked the knowledge that the traits were part of a larger constellation. You may also have felt you were going crazy since your parent's actions and reactions didn't seem predictable or sensible, reasonable or rational. Or you may have felt responsible for triggering your parent's behavior, that if you were better behaved, cuter, smarter, quieter, better at anticipating your parent's needs, that things would be better. You had no way of knowing what the problem was or that it had nothing to do with you.

Discoveries and Reactions

Adult children of parents with BPD may learn about BPD in a variety of ways. Some say they've read a newspaper or magazine article that reminded them of their parent's behavior. Some have learned about BPD in the course of their own therapy, often for issues related to relationships and poor self-esteem, where a counselor recognizes the symptoms. Others say they recognized their parent's BPD through college psychology classes, World Wide Web searches of a parent's symptoms, hospital staff, or friends and relatives who work in the mental health field. But even if your parent has never been formally diagnosed with BPD, if the symptoms and behaviors strike a chord and the effects described in this book fit your experience, you'll be able to benefit from reading further.

Upon learning about BPD, you may feel an incredible sense of relief at finally understanding that you weren't the cause of the inconsistent, perhaps abusive behavior. There was some other explanation for what you experienced. You may feel joy at finally receiving validation and learning that your parent's troubling behavior was indeed real, unhealthy, and that you weren't alone.

Other reactions include denial—"Oh, it wasn't *that* bad;" "I wasn't hit *that* hard," or "*that* often," or "criticized *that* much"—and rationalization. You may find yourself thinking, "But my father/mother had such a traumatic childhood, he/she doesn't know any better." And that may indeed be true. About three-fourths of those with BPD experienced some type of early trauma. Still, that doesn't condone the actions of a parent toward a child. Many people have difficult childhoods; many people don't get the unconditional love and support that children deserve. But many still go on to be healthy, loving parents. More importantly, the possible reasons behind your parent's emotional difficulties don't negate or minimize the truth of your own experience.

Hope for Change

Upon learning about BPD and identifying the ways it's influenced your development and outlook, you may be overwhelmed with a multitude of emotions, including happiness, anger, sadness, grief, and confusion. Those emotions are healthy and understandable, and they will help you move forward. Remember that it is possible to make changes in your life, and that you have the power to do so. It's indeed possible to recast the messages you received as a child, to look at your life through a new lens, and to learn to do things differently. It may not be easy, but it's feasible once you set your mind to it. It's as if you've been an ice-skater all your life, and suddenly someone hands you a new pair of roller skates. You want to learn to use them, so you put them on, and you wobble and fall. But you continue to try to stand up and skate. Each day you wobble less, and after a while, you hardly fall at all. Soon you're skating backwards and doing figure eights—it becomes almost as effortless as skating in your old ice skates. You've learned a new way.

STOP AND THINK: Motivation

Think about your motivation for change. What do you stand to gain in terms of insight and understanding, and improved relationships with your self and others?

Consider your reasons for reading this book and doing the exercises. Perhaps you're hurting or thinking, feeling, or doing things that interfere with your relationships and your sense of contentment. What are those thoughts, feelings or behaviors you'd like to understand and challenge?

What else do you hope to accomplish by reading this book?

The Need to Grieve

Among the myriad emotions you're likely to experience when thinking about your childhood, grief may be chief among them. There are numerous losses associated with learning that someone as important to you as a parent struggles with mental and emotional challenges. Grief is a normal and natural response to loss, such as the death of a loved one. It is also possible to grieve in response to a figurative death, such as the loss of a relationship or the loss of the hopes and expectations you had for a relationship.

For adult children of a parent with emotional deficits, this is a common experience. They grieve for what they never had, or what they may have had only periodically: a stable, validating, and reliable caretaker who allowed them to consistently feel loved, accepted, valued, and respected.

Adult children may grieve for a lost childhood, since they may have assumed the role of a miniature adult and parent to their parent. Parentified children, raised by their parents to be the caretakers, have to grow up quickly, seemingly bypassing the years when children are playful, free, and curious. As adults, they may feel old, tired, and have few memories of their childhood.

Adult children may also grieve over the realization that they may not have been loved for who they were; instead love was conditional, based on looks, intelligence, behavior, or a parent's whim. In *Drama of the Gifted Child*, Alice Miller writes:

> It is one of the turning points in therapy when the patient comes to the emotional insight that all the love she has captured with so much effort and self-denial was not meant for her as she really was, that the admiration for her beauty and achievements

was aimed at this beauty and these achievements and not at the child herself. In therapy, the small and lonely child that is hidden behind her achievements wakes up and asks: "What would have happened if I had appeared before you sad, needy, angry, furious? Where would your love have been then? And I was all these things as well. Does this mean that it was not really me you loved, but only what I pretended to be? The well-behaved, reliable, empathic, understanding, and convenient child, who in fact was never a child at all? What became of my childhood? Have I not been cheated out of it? I can never return to it. I can never make up for it." (1996, p. 39)

Adult children may grieve too for the loss of their own false self, the mask they learned to wear to secure a parent's love. After a while, the mask becomes nearly indistinguishable, even to the child who's wearing it, and the thought of removing it to reveal the real self underneath can be overwhelming. "Who am I if I'm not my father's [or mother's] little girl?" "Who am I if I'm sad, needy, angry, furious?"

Adult children may grieve over the idealized mother or father they never had. They may grieve at suddenly understanding that even if they thought they had a close relationship, it may have been due to the mask they wore, to how they focused on a parent's needs and denied their own.

Adult children may grieve for their parent, who likely experienced trauma and/or didn't receive unconditional love, acceptance, or validation himself. And they may grieve as they watch their parent struggle with BPD. "I wouldn't wish this [disorder] on my worst enemy," said one man about his mother. "For her to act the way she does, she can't feel good about herself. There's no way she could possibly be happy or feel secure. Yeah, I feel robbed at times, but I still feel sad for her because I know she's been robbed too."

Finally, adult children may grieve over their disillusionment with the other parent for not protecting them, saving them, or for not validating their experience with the abusive or neglectful parent. "My father in effect threw us to the wolves," says Johanna, who had a mother with BPD. "He kowtowed to her, to the point of defending her after she'd said something horrible to one of us—'Oh, she didn't really mean it,' or 'Well, you really *shouldn't* have done (or said) that to her.' I'm sure he did that to keep the peace, but I wish he had stood up for us. I mean, we were children, his children, and he was the parent—wasn't that his responsibility?" Others may grieve for the nonborderline parent who left the home or for a parent who was unable to protect them due to her own mental health issues or other reasons.

Dealing with Grief

When it comes to dealing with grief, there's no magic formula. Everyone grieves differently, for varying periods of time. There's no finish line for grief. You may go for months or years thinking you've dealt with your feelings, only to be reminded by a memory, a photograph, something someone says to you, that you're not quite done yet. "When I see certain movies or a mother being very patient and loving toward her child, I'm sometimes sad about what might have been," says Patricia, who has a mother diagnosed with BPD. "I accept that this is the way things are and they can't change. I know that I'll never have a real mother. I've done a lot of work on this issue. But I'm still sad sometimes."

In her seminal work on grief, *On Death and Dying,* psychiatrist Elisabeth Kübler-Ross (1997) identified five stages that define the path to acceptance of death: denial, anger, bargaining, depression, and acceptance. The stages don't occur in a precise order, to the same degree or for the same length of time. Grief is a long process and one that's unique to each of us.

There are parallels to the grief you experience for the death of a living relationship—where the person is not only alive but a part of your life in some way—yet you also grieve for the dashed hope, the deflated expectations, the disappointment at realizing you won't ever have the relationship with your parent that you envisioned (or that society has envisioned for you).

As you continue to read and work through grief, it's important to have someone to work with—a therapist or a trusted, insightful friend—or at the very least, a journal you contribute to often. The feelings can be overwhelming at times, and many adult children report sinking into a deep depression upon learning about their parent's illness and beginning to work through the accompanying emotions. (If this happens to you, it's important that you seek professional help.)

One of the challenges to grieving are the beliefs you may hold about loss. Think about the lessons you learned about loss as a child: if you lost a dog, you may have gleaned that it's okay to cry a little, but that you should also bury the dog, get a new one, and get over it. If you lost a favorite stuffed animal or a friend disappointed you, you may have learned that "these things happen" or that "big kids don't cry." "Get over it," "Don't dwell on the negative," "Put on a happy face and you'll feel better," "The past is the past, and there's nothing you can do about it now" are all messages you may have internalized. If you lost faith in a favorite teacher or another adult disappointed you, the message you may have gotten loud and clear was not to trust adults or have such high expectations.

Here are some other messages you may have received about loss:

- ◇ Bury your feelings; your feelings are too strong or unreasonable; no one else has them.

- ◇ Replace the loss; find someone (or something) else who can give you what you want.

- ◇ Grieve alone; no one wants to hear about your grief—it's depressing and sounds like whining. People will think you're weak.

- ◇ Just give it time; you'll get over it if you don't dwell on it.

STOP AND THINK: Messages about Loss

Which of the above messages about grief and loss have you heard from family, friends, the media and/or have come to believe yourself? What other beliefs about grief and loss do you hold, and where do you think they came from?

Telling It Like It Is

When faced with a person's grief, most well-meaning friends and relatives want you to take their advice so they can feel more effective. They want you to keep your sense of optimism, and they think that denying or keeping busy to avoid painful feelings helps. But dealing with grief is about improving your ability to communicate the truth, to yourself first and foremost.

STOP AND THINK: Revealing the Truth

Itemize the losses you experienced with your parent. Using a time line or a log format in your journal, mentally scan your life for perceived losses. What are you grieving for? For example, "I'm grieving for the childhood I missed. I shouldn't have had to cook and clean for my drunk, depressed parent when I was eleven" or "I'm grieving because my mother is too disruptive to be invited to my upcoming wedding."

Note what feelings are associated with each loss. In the examples above, accompanying emotions might include anger, resentment, sadness.

Have some of your earlier beliefs about grief lead you to deny your feelings? If so, how will you think about your emotions differently now?

There are different ways of coming to terms with loss. Some of the exercises below may help. Do all of them, or choose the one(s) that you think will be most effective for you.

1. Write a letter (which you won't necessarily send) to your parent telling your truth. Explain the reasons for your grief and how you feel. Some of your points may include

   - what you experienced emotionally growing up

   - what you needed and wanted

   - positive interactions (reinforce the positive)

   - making amends for anything you wish you could have said or done differently

   - expressing acceptance for what was and is, and acknowledgement of the limitations your parent may have had

   - identifying realistic expectations about the relationship

   - the emotions and issues you're experiencing as an adult in response to your childhood experience.

2. You're asked to write the eulogy for your parent's funeral (you can do this exercise even if your parent is alive). Without regard for diplomacy or reprisals from other relatives, write your truth.

3. You're asked to write a eulogy for your ideal parent's funeral. Write about the feelings associated with the loss of your expectations, hopes, and wishes.

After doing one or more of the above exercises, design a spiritual ceremony that will be meaningful to you to mark the figurative death of the relationship as you knew it (and/or as you may have wished it). For example, you could take the eulogy for your ideal parent (the third exercise), light a candle memorializing his/her loss and then bury the letter.

Acceptance: Coming to Terms with BPD

It may sound overly simplistic or obvious, but in order to move beyond suffering in any area of your life, you must accept the situation as it is, whether you like it or not, think it's fair or not, whether you have the power to change the circumstances or not. This concept of acceptance is based in Buddhist beliefs. Psychologist Marsha Linehan suggests that acceptance is "the way to turn suffering that cannot be tolerated into pain that can be tolerated. Pain is part of living; it can be emotional and it can be physical. Pain is nature's way of signaling that something is wrong, or that something needs to be done" (Linehan 1993b, p. 102).

STOP AND THINK: Painful Signals

Consider the following examples of how pain may be a healthy response, indicating to you that something needs to change:

- You were so busy this morning, you forgot to eat breakfast. Now it's 1 P.M. and you're getting a headache.

- After yet another exchange of hurtful insults with your girlfriend, you walk away with a lump in your throat and tightness in your chest.

Can you think of examples in your life when physical or emotional pain has been trying to tell you something?

What was your reaction to the pain? Did your reaction serve you well? If you denied the pain, what were the results?

Acceptance doesn't mean you approve; it doesn't mean you're happy about something; it doesn't mean you won't work to change the situation or your response to it, but it does mean that you *acknowledge* reality as it is—with all its sadness, humor, irony, and gifts—at a particular point in time.

Imagine you're taking a calculus course, and struggling with the homework assignments. But you deny that you're having trouble. What happens? You fall further behind and your frustration increases. If, on the other hand, you accept that you're having a hard time, you can change. You can ask the instructor for help. You can buy an additional textbook. You can now start to make some improvement. Your acceptance, your acknowledgment is the first step.

STOP AND THINK: Acceptance as Impetus

What are the issues with your borderline parent that continue to cause you pain? List them in your journal.

Now write a statement for each item you listed to acknowledge that it's a continuing source of suffering. For example: "I recognize that it still hurts when I think I'll never have the mother-daughter relationship some of my friends talk about."

Facing the Stigma

Coming to terms with the realization that a parent may have had BPD means facing the stigma of mental illness—not a pretty topic by society's standards. In fact it's one that's often the butt of jokes, the subject of gossip, or simply ignored because it makes people uncomfortable. And of all mental illnesses, BPD is one of the most stigmatized, perhaps because the disorder often involves difficulty with anger, volatility, and mood swings. Loved ones feel helpless, and clinicians don't always identify the disorder. When they do, some don't want to treat it.

What about Me?

Many adult children wonder whether they might have the disorder as well. Chances are good that if you're even asking the question, you don't, since those with the disorder often find it very difficult to take ownership of their thoughts, feelings, and actions. As Simon, thirty-four, says, "My father thought he was perfectly fine—it was just the rest of the world that was crazy." And while studies have shown that genetics plays a role in the development of BPD, your DNA alone does not dictate whether it will unfold; it takes a complex interplay of factors.

Still, being raised by a parent with perhaps severe emotional challenges and limitations may indeed have taught you some maladaptive ways of seeing the world, of coping with distress, of relating to yourself and to others. Acknowledging this, identifying those beliefs and behaviors, and then making changes can seem daunting.

Coming to terms with a parent's illness can also be extremely painful because adult children may see aspects of their parent in themselves. You've probably heard people joke that as they get older they've become "just like my mother (or father)." On a serious note, adult children may see their parent's eyes or other facial feature each time they look in the mirror, see their parent's hands when they look at their own, hear their parent's voice when they speak, or see familiar mannerisms in their own movements and expressions. "I've worked so hard to exorcise him from my life," says Simon, "but every time I look in the mirror—we have the same eyes and mouth—I can't help but see him."

Making Sense of Opposites

Facing the truth about a parent's emotional challenges may also be difficult for adult children because it entails acceptance of what may seem like polar opposites. A parent who was cruel or neglectful some or even much of the time may also have had moments when she provided love and comfort. This may cause you to question your experience since it's hard to believe that a parent, who in some circumstances seemed functional, was also capable of inflicting extreme physical or emotional pain in other circumstances. "I guess it wasn't all bad. She could be a raging ogre, and I'd hide in the closet so she wouldn't find me, but, you know, sometimes she was a good mother," says Deborah, a forty-three-year-old woman. "She'd play with me or let me have friends over, and I do remember her giving me hugs sometimes." For adult children who witnessed the black-and-white thinking or splitting of BPD, reconciling the two extremes may prove especially difficult.

STOP AND THINK: Exploring Extremes

Think of a situation in which you yourself had quite different or seemingly opposing reactions or feelings. What were the reasons (was it related to your thoughts, to the person or people involved, or something else about the context, for example)?

Now imagine your reactions amplified by a factor of ten, or one hundred. How do you think you'd feel?

The purpose of this exercise is to help you gain some insight into how your parent might have been feeling during a situation where he showed a seemingly contradictory or opposing reaction. Everyone has some fluctuations in how they respond to circumstances they find stressful, but for someone with BPD, who already tends toward extremes, the fluctuation is magnified and sometimes has very little to do with the situation at hand. This isn't to excuse the behavior, rather to help you understand what you may have experienced.

Banishing Self-Blame

Part of accepting a parent's affliction is understanding that how you were treated as a child wasn't your fault; it had nothing to do with you being bad, but was about the disorder and the parent's issues. Yet it's extremely difficult to avoid self-blame. Children need to believe their parents will nurture and protect them. If the parents don't nurture and protect, if they are physically or emotionally abusive, if they blame the child for their or the family's problems, their children are left to believe it's due to some inherent flaw in them rather than the parent's deficits. To a child, who derives most everything but the air she breathes from her mother and/or father, it's unthinkable to her that the parent can't meet her needs—it must be her fault. The thought pattern begins in infancy and is reinforced throughout childhood, leading to profound feelings of shame and self-blame.

STOP AND THINK: Banishing Self-Blame

In *Children of the Self-Absorbed*, Nina Brown explains that even though a narcissistic parent may blame her adult child, you don't need to blame yourself for "not being perfect; failing to anticipate your parent's needs or wants; appropriately meeting your own needs; being different or less satisfying than others; disappointing your parent" (p. 87).

On a scale of 1 to 5 (1 being "not at all" and 5 being "very much") evaluate how much you blame yourself for

_____ being less than perfect

_____ failing to satisfy your parent's needs, desires, or expectations

_____ asking for what you need

_____ seeing and telling the truth

_____ disappointing a parent

_____ situations beyond your control, such as a family member's illness or financial strains

Now consider to what degree you subscribe to the following beliefs using the same 1 to 5 scale:

____ If I had said/done . . . I could have changed my parent's beliefs about me.

____ My parent will accept me if I would only change . . .

____ My parent will change.

____ My parent ultimately knows what's best for me. If I don't meet his/her expectations, I'll never be satisfied with myself.

____ Deep down, I know I'm defective in some way.

____ I deserve to feel the shame I feel.

____ If I explain how I feel to my parent the right way, I'll be able to help him/her change.

____ If I were just more loving toward my parents, they'd come around.

Now take each of the above beliefs for which you answered with a 2 or higher and challenge it. Write your responses in your journal. For example, using the first belief: "If I had said/done . . . I could have changed my parent's beliefs about me," your challenge might be: "There is nothing I could have said or done—or could say or do today—that would have changed my parent." Or "Even if I had been the world's most perfect child, my parent would have found fault with something because it wasn't about me at all—it was about him."

While it's indeed possible for those with BPD to change their feelings, beliefs, and behaviors, it's not likely, especially after so many years. As you try to accept your situation and move beyond it, you must give up the hope, the fantasy, the wish, that your parent will change significantly. Think of it this way: If they do change, it will be a wonderful gift, a bonus, *but it's not something you can realistically expect.*

Feeling What You Feel

Yet another challenge of coming to terms with a parent's mental illness may be feeling and accepting your own emotions. It's not uncommon for parents with BPD to deny or invalidate the emotions of others when they perceive those emotions as threatening. Adult children often remember how they weren't allowed to express feelings. As a result of keeping your emotions bottled up for years, you may have come to block them, hide

them, deny them, numb out with food, drugs, or alcohol, and you may
have trouble

- ◊ identifying your emotions

- ◊ recognizing when you're beginning to feel an emotion

- ◊ experiencing an emotion

- ◊ accepting that you feel an emotion

- ◊ trusting yourself to express your feelings to others

- ◊ feeling safe to express emotions to others

You may also have trouble managing your emotions.

- ◊ Do you feel that you're controlled by your emotions?

- ◊ Do you feel out of control when you're feeling upset, anxious, angry, or sad?

- ◊ Do your emotions sometimes feel like they'll last forever?

- ◊ Do you say or do things when you're very emotional that you regret later?

- ◊ Do you wish you could tame your emotions or perhaps be unemotional at times?

STOP AND THINK: Emotional Challenges

What are some of your emotional challenges? Where do you think these
issues came from?

Set a few goals for recognizing and managing your emotions. What
do you want to work on improving? Commit them to paper, and think
about how you'll judge improvement. For instance, "I know I'll be more
in control of my feelings when I can say why I'm angry rather than immediately start yelling."

Emotional Shades of Meaning

There are hundreds of emotions, ranging in degree and sometimes
with only subtle differences between them. For instance, anger can range
from mild irritation or annoyance to rage and fury; sadness can range
from feeling a little blue to utter despair and hopelessness. It's important
to understand the distinctions among emotions as well as to be able to
assess how you feel. Because you feel annoyed with someone doesn't mean

you should fly into a rage and swear never to speak to them again. Because you feel sad about something that happened today doesn't mean the world will end and you should give up all hope of ever feeling better. Emotion *dys*regulation is a hallmark of BPD, and children raised by a parent with it may not have had the best emotional role model to learn from.

Emotions serve several purposes, actually. They help you communicate with yourself and with others, they serve your need to influence and control your environment and the behavior of others, they alert you to danger, they help organize and motivate you for action, and they validate your perceptions of the world around you.

Your emotional life is shaped by many factors, including your biology and temperament and the external responses you receive from others. You're also influenced by your thoughts and feelings, such as your interpretation of an experience. For instance, a loud, unexpected noise may sound like an explosion in one context or like a harmless street construction project in another. Emotions can also be caused by other, primary, emotions, such as when hurt or disappointment leads to anger or when anger leads to feelings of guilt. Finally, your beliefs influence your emotional life. As discussed with grief and self-blame, it's important to identify the beliefs you may hold about emotions and challenge them.

STOP AND THINK:
Common Beliefs about Emotions

Mark the statements below with which you agree. Consider to what degree you've incorporated them into your emotional life. Then try to write a statement that transforms each one into a healthier belief.

_____ If I share my emotions with the people around me, they'll think I'm weak, or worse, crazy.

_____ There are right and wrong ways I should feel, depending on the circumstance.

_____ Someone who's really emotional is probably out of control a lot of the time.

_____ If I spend too much time analyzing my emotions, I'll come across to others as self-absorbed.

_____ It's generally safer not to talk too much about emotions; no one will understand anyway.

_____ When I feel angry (jealous, hurt), I should be able to just snap out of it.

_____ Emotions are unproductive. After all, they don't really mean anything.

_____ Negative emotions are usually the result of something else, like PMS or waking up on the wrong side of the bed; they're not really valid and they change for no reason.

Think about what other beliefs about emotions you hold. Now, for each one, write a statement that challenges it.

Recognizing Emotions

If emotions are dynamic and subjective, how can you recognize them? How can you identify what you're feeling? At times you may know right away. At other times, you may figure it out based on your actions. For example, you may suddenly realize your voice is getting louder, and you'd understand you were feeling anger. Our thoughts can also tell us about our emotions—"I realized all these morbid thoughts were running through my mind, and I knew I was feeling sad." And physical sensations can signal emotions: a racing heart, tight muscles, tightness in your chest, clenched fists or jaw, shaking hands, ringing ears, flushed cheeks, pounding temples, tears, sweaty palms, or relaxed shoulders for example.

STOP AND THINK: What Are Your Signs?

What cognitive signs (thoughts), actions, and physical signals indicate particular emotions for you? Write them down in your journal. Be sure to include signs for anger, sadness, fear, anxiety, and happiness.

Accepting Painful Emotions

Next time you realize you're beginning to feel a strong emotion, try to just pay attention to it without judging yourself for having it ("I shouldn't be angry about this; it wasn't really his fault") or react to it (verbally attacking the person you're angry at). Try not to deny the emotion ("It's fine; I'm not angry"). Instead, be aware of it and how you feel. Don't assume you're overreacting or misinterpreting the situation.

Expect this to be extremely difficult. Try not to take action based on your feelings until after you've been able to pay attention to them for a while. And remember that the intensity *will* pass, and you can address the situation later.

Make It Easier to Manage Your Emotions

It's not possible—or desirable—to eliminate distressing emotions, but they're a whole lot easier to accept and manage when you know you possess the ability to nurture yourself and feel rested, clearheaded, healthy, and strong.

Circumstances will inevitably arise that you can't control, such as the weather, accidents, other people's behavior. But more often than not, you have quite a bit of control over how you respond to your feelings. The following may seem obvious, but they're very easy to overlook:

◊ Get the right amount of rest—neither too much nor too little. If you have trouble sleeping, you should be evaluated by a sleep specialist. Commonly prescribed medications, alcohol, eating before bed, stress, sleep apnea, and other factors and conditions can affect sleep patterns and subsequently how you feel during waking hours. Getting too much sleep can make you feel groggy and sluggish.

◊ Take good care of yourself physically. Follow preventive care regimens and seek treatment for any conditions you may have.

◊ Eat a healthy, balanced diet. If you have food restrictions based on physical conditions (allergies or diabetes, for instance), be sure to adhere to them.

◊ Exercise. Set realistic goals for yourself, based on your current state of health. If you've been sedentary, don't set a goal of running a marathon in the coming six months. Rather, for instance, aim for a ten-minute walk three days a week for a month, then four days a week, then five days a week, then try walking for fifteen minutes at a time.

◊ Reduce or avoid substances such as alcohol, marijuana, cocaine, caffeine. Take prescription medications only under the care of your physician and/or psychiatrist.

◊ Do things that help you feel confident and competent, as seemingly small as they may be.

◊ Don't isolate yourself. Call or visit with friends on a regular basis.

◊ Make a list of some simple things that make you feel happy and appreciative (looking at a flower, lighting a candle, listening to a favorite song or CD, reading before getting out of bed in the morning) and try to do at least one of them daily.

Telling Your Truth to Family and Friends

Part of accepting the reality of your parent's shortcomings and your own circumstances is communicating your history and feelings to those close to you. As you find out about this illness and its impact on you, it's only natural to want to confide in others. At the same time, you should be aware that others may resist hearing what you have to say and may make invalidating comments. In an ideal world, we would all get enthusiastic validation from others when we disclose personal information, but unfortunately it's not an ideal world. And because you grew up not having your feelings and perceptions acknowledged and mirrored, you may be especially sensitive to invalidation from others around you.

Invalidation

Have you ever confided in a friend about a touchy family situation or your suspicion that your parent had BPD, only to hear, "Oh, I'm sure it wasn't that bad," or, "But your father/mother is so nice, he/she probably didn't mean it the way you think"? It can be maddening, saddening, frustrating, and terribly disappointing to have your feelings and perceptions dismissed by someone you thought understood you, who you trusted enough to confide in. But the other person's reaction doesn't negate your perceptions. Because someone doesn't agree with you or understand what you're conveying doesn't mean you're wrong.

Consider some of the reasons why a person might make invalidating comments. They include society's beliefs and myths about family and kinship:

◊ Blood is thicker than water.

◊ Honor thy parents.

◊ Love conquers all.

◊ Keep the peace.

◊ Don't air dirty laundry.

◊ What will the neighbors think?

Can you think of other beliefs, myths, and sayings?

Because many consider discussions of "what goes on behind closed doors" to be off-limits in social settings, some people just may be uncomfortable talking about family dysfunction and highly emotional issues. They may therefore not have much experience and may not really know how to be a good listener or how to validate what someone else says. They may truly be intending to help, provide feedback, or offer solutions, even though you may not perceive it that way.

Everybody has issues to come to terms with. You never really know as you tell someone else *your* story what thoughts, emotions, and painful memories it's raising for them. Even if others don't tell you—and they may not realize themselves—your words may hit a little too close to home. Their reaction may in fact have very little to do with your disclosures and more with their own insecurities, fears, and projections.

A Rule of Disclosure

Remember that you're not obligated to share information with anyone you don't want to. It's easy to be seduced, if you will, by someone who seems to demonstrate the qualities you so desperately wanted (want) in a parent. So when an acquaintance or friend appears to be interested in you and your life, it's very tempting to quickly open up and share personal details. A good rule-of-thumb is to disclose information slowly. Keep in mind the analogy of getting accustomed to a pool of cold water. You first dip your toe in, then wade up to your knees for a while, then perhaps splash a little water on your arms and torso before diving in. No matter how well you know someone, it's entirely up to you to decide how much, if anything, you want to disclose.

STOP AND THINK:
Minimizing the Risk of Invalidation

Make a list of the qualities and/or behaviors that make you feel comfortable confiding in someone. For example, you might list things like "doesn't interrupt, doesn't gossip, is sensitive and empathetic."

Now make a list of the behaviors and qualities that would serve as a warning to you that a person might not be someone with whom you want to share sensitive information. You might list things like, "gossips a lot, cuts me off mid-sentence with, 'That's nothing, you should hear what happened to me.'"

The above exercise may cause you to think further about who your real friends are. It's important at different points in your life to consider that. As you grow and change and develop more insight, your friends will likely change too. You may find that you've outgrown certain friendships. You may come to realize someone you were close to now reminds you in some important ways of your parent with BPD. You may begin to notice that you're not as excited to spend time with some people as you used to be, or that you become bored or tired as you interact with them. Again, it's up to you to choose your friends. Because someone wants to be your friend or says he needs you doesn't mean the relationship works for you. It's entirely your choice.

If you're with someone you don't want to share information with, or you get into a conversation and realize you're not comfortable sharing anything further, it's perfectly acceptable to say, "You know, that's just not something I want to talk about now," or "I really don't feel like getting into it today," or "It's complicated."

STOP AND THINK: Putting on the Brakes

Using your own words and personal style, come up with three to five statements that firmly but politely make it clear that you won't be sharing further details. Remember too that communication relies heavily on body language and voice inflection, so practice your statements (in front of a mirror or with a friend or therapist) standing up straight, looking directly at the person, and finishing your statement deliberately so that it doesn't sound timid or like you're asking for permission.

Develop and rehearse some responses to invalidating remarks you've heard. Some examples to develop, rehearse, and then file away might include, "I realize that's your experience, but mine tells me something different," or "I understand that outsiders might not see it this way, but I know what I know." While it's good to do this so you don't feel like kicking yourself later for what you think you should have said, you also don't want to walk around constantly on guard, assuming others *won't* accept what you have to say.

Family Investments

Sharing your experience with a borderline parent may present different or additional challenges when you broach the subject with family members, who are obviously more invested in what you have to say than people who aren't related. Family members may

- ◊ wonder if your parent's illness was somehow their fault or whether they contributed in some way

- ◊ be upset with themselves for not realizing something was wrong

- ◊ be angry, sad, disappointed that their hopes and expectations were dashed

- ◊ feel guilty for not doing more to protect you and your siblings

- ◊ be frightened that they have or will develop borderline traits themselves

- ◊ suffer from something akin to survivor's guilt, where they wonder why they didn't develop the disorder but your parent did

When invalidation comes from a family member, it can be devastating. Dan, the grown son of a mother he believes has BPD, recalls telling his mother's sister about the disorder. He'd just learned about it in an Internet forum—the symptoms and stories he read fit his experience so closely "it was scary." Feeling a tremendous sense of relief at finally understanding what he experienced during his childhood, he told a few relatives, including his aunt. She listened but didn't say much, but later he found out through his sister that his aunt thought he was lying. "She asked my sister how I could be such a lout and 'stir up all this trouble' when 'clearly it wasn't true.'"

In the face of such comments from loved ones, it may help to think about what their interest is in denying the issues you've raised. It also may help to remember that not everyone has had the same experience with your parent that you have. As discussed earlier, a parent with BPD or its traits may split siblings, treating one as the angelic favorite and another as the cause of all evil. Perceptions of childhood will look very different depending on your perspective. Other relatives, particularly siblings, may also still be enmeshed with the parent, so caught up in their relationship with the parent that they won't—they can't—question the dynamics. Remember though, that you know what you experienced. Because someone sees it differently or questions your interpretation doesn't make you wrong. It doesn't lessen your feelings; it doesn't change your truth.

PART 2

The Present

CHAPTER 4

Guilt, Responsibility, and Forgiveness

Guilt. It's a word often heard among adult children of parents with BPD, but what does it really refer to? Guilt is often confused with shame, but in fact they're two different things. Guilt is an emotion; it's the feeling that you've done something wrong. According to author John Bradshaw, "healthy guilt is the emotional core of our conscience. It is emotion which results from behaving in a certain manner contrary to our beliefs and values. Guilt presupposes internalized rules and develops later [in life] than shame. . . . Guilt does not reflect directly upon one's identity or diminish one's sense of personal worth" (1988, p. 17). Thought of in those terms, feeling guilty would be a healthy response if you believe shoplifting is wrong, but for some reason you do it anyway. You've behaved contrary to your beliefs and values; you've violated your internal rules.

Why Do You Feel Guilty?

While guilt can be a healthy response, *toxic* guilt is another story. Guilt that you don't process, guilty thoughts that you let churn over and over in your mind, leads to internalized guilt and the sense that you're responsible for things that you couldn't possibly be responsible for. This kind of guilt is common for adult children of a parent with BPD. So where does it come from?

A sense of guilt may have its origins in any one or a combination of the following:

The need to feel you are in control. A sense of immense responsibility may be a means to feel powerful and in control of a situation where you feel powerless and out of control (Bradshaw 1988). For example, a girl feels responsible for her father's repeated suicide attempts. She may be too young to realize that what her father does is his own choice. She also lives in constant fear because she never knows when she might come home from school and find him close to death or worse. Guilt and a sense of responsibility actually may allow her to feel like she has some control over her unstable home life.

The roles you play, or used to play, within your family. When you begin to remove your assigned mask, refuse to maintain the charade, or perhaps even speak out to others about your experience, you may feel guilty for violating the pact, albeit silently and implicitly agreed upon, and exposing others. For example, the man who was seen as the all-good child by his borderline mother may feel guilty as he begins therapy sessions and talks about his childhood. As a boy, he was the caretaker, his mother's friend, and he has to struggle not to feel like he's betraying her when he talks to his therapist and thinks critically about his experience.

Weak boundaries and projective identification. When you're enmeshed with someone else, when your boundaries aren't clearly defined, it's hard to judge where your obligations and responsibilities end and your parent's begin. A parent may unconsciously project her guilty feelings onto her child; in order to avoid feeling guilty, which is common in BPD, it's particularly easy for a child to identify with the projection and feel guilty *for* the parent. This is called *projective identification,* and here's an example of how it works: A woman is feeling especially short-tempered and impatient with her young child one day. When the child says, "I'm hungry, can I have lunch now?" the woman loses her cool and screams, "I can't believe how incredibly selfish you are. Can't you see that it's not lunchtime yet?" The woman is projecting; what she really is conveying indirectly is, "I'm fried. I don't feel like I can handle one more thing, like making lunch, right now. But I must be selfish to feel that way, and I can't accept my own emotions, so I'm going to say they're coming from you, that it's your fault." The child, who believes what Mom tells her and who is trying to understand why she got yelled at for something as logical as requesting food when she was hungry, assumes that a) she's responsible for her mother's reaction; and b) she's selfish to boot. She incorporates that knowledge and toxic guilt accumulates.

How Guilt Works

Adult children may wonder whether their borderline parent uses guilt consciously and deliberately, since it may feel that way. We'll talk more about a parent's accountability shortly, but *whether they do so consciously or unconsciously*, people with emotional challenges may induce feelings of guilt in others through their attempts to

- ◊ control their own environment and minimize unknowns

- ◊ illicit a desired result from others or a desired outcome to a situation

- ◊ avoid taking responsibility for their actions, accepting their own feelings, or facing their own thoughts

Given the myriad emotions you may feel when reflecting on your formative years and the complexity of your experience, it may be extremely difficult to tease out the origins of your guilty feelings. Guilt can operate in very subtle ways within a family, and how it works may not be obvious from just a few memorable incidents. In fact, it may be that numerous yet seemingly benign experiences reinforced your feelings over the course of time.

The following are some of the ways in which adult children of parents with BPD may come to feel overly guilty and responsible:

Having a different perception of reality. It's not okay to see things differently; borderline parents impose their perceptions on others as the *right* way. For instance, Micah, an adult child, offers to help his parents paint their living room *if* he's available and not too tired on a particular weekend. His parents hear (because they want to), "I'll definitely help you paint the living room." As the weekend approaches, Micah decides he's not up to the task and lets his parents know he won't be able to help. His parents respond, "Oh, but Micah, we were counting on you to come through. You said you would. How will we get it done without you?"

Criticism and accusations. Relentless disapproval by a parent and misplaced blame can lead to feelings of guilt. If you constantly hear that you've ruined something, that you've acted inappropriately, that you shouldn't have done something (or should have done something and didn't), that "you always...," you're likely to begin to believe that you're responsible and that you let others down. You may even start to question whether you did some of the things you were accused of but somehow you forgot, so convincing is your parent's belief in your guilt!

Finding yourself in no-win situations. No matter what you do, you're wrong. For example, if you defend yourself against an accusation, your parent may ask why you're "so defensive," or tell you to lighten up, or to stop being so sensitive. If you don't defend yourself, he may interpret your silence as an admission of guilt and validation of his perception. Either way, you lose. And you start to feel that you must be responsible and guilty. Lily recalls being accused on several occasions of things she didn't do. She would cry in frustration at being suspect and not being believed when she told the truth. Her mother would say tauntingly, "What's the matter—you crying because I caught you? You, my dear, have a guilty conscience." In another case, Cheryl recalls her mother's recent birthday. "She told me not to buy her a gift—she wanted me to save my money and put it toward decorating my new house. Her birthday came, and I sent a nice card and called her. She was sullen on the phone and said, 'The card was nice, but I was a little disappointed. You know, your sister sent me a lovely bouquet of flowers.'"

Denial and projection. The borderline parent denies the effect of his behavior and blames you instead. For instance, a parent may make a cruel joke at your expense and, when you don't laugh, say, "You don't appreciate my sense of humor. Why are you so serious about everything?" Or a parent, when confronted about her frustrating behavior, might project and say something like, "So you think I'm difficult? If you weren't so self-absorbed, you'd see that *you're* the one who's difficult."

Having a parent play the martyr card. You may have heard, or hear, statements such as, "After all I've done for you. . . ," "You don't know all the sacrifices I've made. . . ," "If I had known how you'd end up treating me. . . ," "No matter how horrible you are to me, I'll always love you."

Withholding affection. A parent may hold you responsible for a problem and deny affection, offer up the silent treatment or rage uncontrollably until you've confessed or apologized.

STOP AND THINK: Guilty Feelings

Consider how guilt has operated in your own life and in your relationship with your parent. What are the things for which you feel guilty? List whatever comes to mind, without censoring yourself or thinking, "I know I shouldn't really feel guilty for this. . . ." Some examples include feeling guilty for

- not spending the holidays with your family of origin

- saying no to a parent's request for communication or a visit

- all the sacrifices a parent made over the years for you

- taking pride in your accomplishments

- your parent's outburst of anger last Thanksgiving

- accepting help or gifts from others

- wishing a parent would die, "just go away," or leave you alone permanently.

To prompt your thinking, you might want to do this exercise, adapted from the *Stop Walking on Eggshells Workbook* (Kreger and Shirley 2002). Complete the following thoughts, filling in the blanks from your own experience. Start with "I feel guilty for. . . :"

- thinking or not thinking . . .

- doing or not doing . . .

- feeling or not feeling . . .

- saying or not saying . . .

- believing or not believing . . .

- challenging or not challenging . . .

- having or not having . . .

- behaving or not behaving . . .

- reacting or not reacting . . .

- having been or not having been . . .

For each item you listed, consider why you feel guilty (again, not whether you *should*). How did (does) guilt operate in your family of origin, and how did that facilitate your feelings of responsibility?

Owning Your Own Feelings and Nothing More

One of the positive things about feeling guilty is that you can usually make amends when the feeling is warranted. But how can you know when feelings of guilt are indeed warranted by your actions (or inaction)? It's not easy, as there may be a grain of truth embedded among the accusations or projections of a parent with BPD. For instance, your parent might say, "You always sound angry when you talk to me. Why are you so mad at me? What did I ever do to you?" The parent's statement and questions show an unwillingness to accept responsibility for your anger (employing denial and perhaps projection as a defense), but there may be truth to her observation that you "always sounds angry" when you talk to her.

STOP AND THINK: Am I Guilty?

Sifting through it all can be confusing, but there are several ways you can discern whether your guilt and feelings of responsibility are warranted or whether they are feelings that you can put to rest.

Ask yourself the following questions:

- Is (or was) the criticism aimed at me in proportion to the perceived offense? (Either way, acknowledge that you're human, and humans make mistakes.)

- Did I violate a boundary the other person had communicated to me?

- Did I make a promise or commitment I didn't keep?

- Was I truly responsible? Did I have control over the outcome?

- What was my intention or motivation?

- What does my gut or intuition tell me about the situation and my level of responsibility?

- Given a similar set of circumstances, would my close friends (or someone else you admire) think I was responsible?

- Were any of my words or actions efforts at self-protection or self-preservation?

Other questions to consider include:

- What are the costs of feeling guilty when you're really not responsible? Does it sap your energy or emotional strength, take time away from your family, or affect your health?

- Are there ways in which feeling guilty serves you in your relationship with your parent? Does it make you feel more in control, perhaps? Are there other ways it serves you?

- What do you stand to gain by giving up your feelings of guilt and responsibility?

If you determine that your feelings of guilt are actually warranted, then consider the ways in which you might address and correct your actions. If you determine that some of your feelings of guilt are not warranted, you'll have to work on letting go of them, and not accepting any more blame than your fair share.

Letting Go

Part of being able to let go is to know—really know—that you have no control over what others think. If your father thinks you're the worst child on the planet because you refuse to side with him in a family argument, well, that's not something you can control. And your energy would be better spent on the other concerns in your life. If your mother tells you not to buy her a birthday present, but then says she's disappointed that you didn't send one, that's also not something that warrants your guilt.

You also don't owe anyone an explanation or need to defend yourself against accusations or criticism. A simple, "That's too bad; I'm sorry you feel that way" should suffice. Randi Kreger and Paul Shirley (2002) provide a list of responses you can use when feeling like you need to explain or defend yourself. Here is an adaptation of their list:

- ◊ I'm sorry, I won't be able to.

- ◊ I'm sorry that makes you upset.

- ◊ I just can't do that.

- ◊ I understand you feel that way, but I'm still going to have to say no.

- ◊ That's your choice; this is mine.

- ◊ I know I've done that for you in the past, but this time I can't.

- ◊ You may have a point, but my answer is still no.

- ◊ I know you feel that way, and I hope you find another solution.

You might want to practice these statements in front of a mirror or with a trusted friend or therapist until you're comfortable saying them in your own words, with supporting body language and tone of voice. It may be hard, when faced with an actual situation, to stick to your guns and not say, "Oh, all right, just one last time." But your self-esteem will get a much-deserved boost if you don't accept emotions that aren't your own.

Responsibility

In talking about guilt, you may ask, "If I'm not responsible for my parent's actions and reactions, then who is? Is my parent?" The question of accountability is a complex one; by its nature, BPD makes it that way. People with the disorder may have extreme emotional fluctuations, making their feelings and subsequent actions look confusing, disconnected, and contradictory. They may then feel tremendous guilt and shame, even remorse, and this makes it difficult for them to own their behavior. They may not know how to face their feelings of shame and remorse, or they may lack the insight and emotional acuity to realize the impact they have on others.

You may wonder if your parent was aware of some of the negative things he may have said to you as a child (or as an adult). You may wonder if he knew what he was doing when he locked you and your brother out of the house late at night since he claims he never did such a thing. You may wonder how your mother could have not realized that you didn't have adequate clothing each winter, since she tells stories of how she treated you like a princess. Do they really not remember? Did they rewrite history? Were they aware at the time that what they were doing may have been dangerous, unhealthy, or cruel?

There's no clear-cut answer. And the answers may vary by incident or context. On one occasion, a parent may be so ashamed of his anger that he will project it onto you, vehemently denying all the while that he's angry or that he's projecting. Another time, that same man might dissociate during a rage and later will truly not remember that he broke your car window. Another time, when confronted, he might tell you he does not remember that he said something awful to you when he really does.

One woman says that depending on the day, her mother would sometimes cry when confronted with some of the things she did to her children and say, "You know I loved you. I did the best I could." Other times, when confronted with the very same issues and incidents, her mother would get angry and yell, "You and your sister are oblivious—do you have *any* idea how bratty and difficult you two were?" Another time, the woman recalls, her mother flat out denied that certain events took place, events which she'd previously acknowledged.

Whatever your parent's reaction, the result may be a striking lack of validation of your experience. And if parents aren't willing to own their own behavior, you may be inclined—consciously or unconsciously—to accept responsibility for it, as discussed earlier. You may feel compassion for them, thinking, "But she can't help it, she's sick," or, "He never learned any better from *his* parents." These sentiments are valid. It's also true that no one asks to have BPD; your parent didn't choose it and it's not easy to live with—imagine always feeling ashamed, that people are out to get you, that everything is unsafe and that the people you love may up and leave you at any time. Imagine feeling very fragile and out of control.

Yet those with BPD or any other set of symptoms that impact their functioning and their interactions with others can choose to ignore them or try to manage them. One man likens his mother's refusal to acknowledge and seek help for her symptoms to that of a diabetic who won't skip dessert (or take her insulin). One woman, on an Internet bulletin board, writes:

> *Imagine you knew someone who was physically disabled, but if they worked really hard and went to physical therapy—even though it was lengthy and painful—they would have a good chance of leading a fairly normal life. They would probably be able to walk, run, exercise, play, etc. Now, imagine that person refused to seek help, and instead sat around complaining all day. Imagine they blamed everyone around them for their suffering. Imagine they wanted everyone else to cater to them and take care of them. How much compassion would you have then?*
>
> *I know the nature of BPD makes it difficult to admit they're less than perfect and therefore seek treatment. There are, however, cases of recovered borderlines. It can be done. Our parents choose not to do it. I feel sad that my mom is suffering, but I also know she is the only person that can do anything about it, and she chooses not to. There is nothing I can do, and I don't feel responsible. And I won't allow her to inflict her suffering on me anymore, either.*

If your parent doesn't own his particular behavior, there's little hope for change. According to Kenneth Silk, a professor of psychiatry at the University of Michigan Medical School and editor of two books on the neurobiology of personality disorders,

> *Because treatments are so limited, one of the things [those with BPD] need is to believe they can cope, that they have skills and*

are empowered. They need to be responsible for what they do. I'm not saying they're manipulative or that they don't have very real symptoms. But we all have to make decisions about how we're going to release tension and what the consequences will be. These people have a great tendency to justify what we consider unacceptable behavior and then externalize it and rationalize it. But if they can't own some of their behavior, they can't change. (2002)

From the perspective of the adult child, the most validating experience would be for your parent to acknowledge her behavior and its affect on you, and perhaps even apologize and make changes. It may happen, though it might occur only partially and over a long period of time, with a parent accepting weaknesses in certain areas but denying or rationalizing others. Whether or to what extent this acknowledgement takes place, you have to make a choice: continue to hope your parent will own his feelings and actions, which may prove draining and useless. Or accept your parent's inability to do so at the present time and focus on those things in *your* life that you can change.

Taking Charge of Yourself

When you're in pain, it's very easy to ask yourself who's to blame, who's responsible. This is normal, and it allows you to discharge some of your bad feelings by focusing instead on who's guilty, why, and how terrible they were. But when you blame someone for how you feel, you're also casting yourself in the role of victim (McKay, Rogers, and McKay 1989). This means you've handed quite a lot of power over to another person. In effect you've put your well-being in the other person's hands—probably not a prudent thing to do, given your experience with this person.

Reframing

It may be helpful to reframe your situation with an emotionally challenged person as one of conflicting needs (McKay, Rogers, and McKay 1989). For instance, your parent has a need to project his feelings and deny responsibility for past actions in order to protect his sense of self and minimize the shame he feels. You, on the other hand, have a need for validation of the emotional abuse you suffered and can no longer accept or identify with his projections if you want to live your own (healthy) life. When viewed this way, blame no longer seems so necessary—you are no longer the unwitting victim of the "bad guy." You have a measure of control.

Consider the concepts below about personal responsibility, adapted from McKay, Rogers, and McKay (1989). Keep in mind that these statements may sound radical upon first reading. Also keep in mind that they're not designed to invalidate or minimize your past experience, but rather to help you see your current feelings in a different light.

- ◊ You alone are responsible for the level of satisfaction with the interactions you choose to have.

- ◊ If your strategies for interacting don't work, there's no point in blaming the other person.

- ◊ The best question to ask yourself isn't, "Who's responsible for my pain?" but "What can I do about it?"

- ◊ You can't expect others to change or be any different than they are.

- ◊ Relationships come down to two fundamental choices: adapt or let go.

- ◊ As an adult, you're never a victim (though you may have been a victim as a child, betrayed or neglected by the very people responsible for your care and nurturing).

In a similar vein, in *Creating Love*, John Bradshaw (1992) writes the following, paraphrasing family therapist Virginia Satir:

. . . when people are highly functional, they have five freedoms available to them. They have the freedom to:

- ◊ See and hear what they see and hear rather than what they are supposed to see and hear

- ◊ Think what they think rather than what they are supposed to think

- ◊ Feel what they feel rather than what they are supposed to feel

- ◊ Want what they want rather than what they are supposed to want

- ◊ Imagine what they imagine rather than what they are supposed to imagine (p. 132)

Think of the five freedoms as not only things you're *free* to do, but things you're *responsible* to yourself to do!

STOP AND THINK: Taking Ownership

Complete the following statements about your sense of ownership of your own thoughts, feelings, actions, and reactions. There are no right or wrong answers; just fill in the blanks with the thoughts that come to mind:

- I have the right to think. . . , no matter what anyone says about it.

- I have the right to feel. . . , no matter what anyone says about it.

- I have the right to act. . . , no matter what anyone says about it.

- I may not have control over . . . , but I do have control over. . . .

- I have the ability to make choices about. . . .

- When I. . . , I feel in control of my own life.

Note how you feel after completing these statements. Do you feel scared, relieved, angry? Write about your reactions in your journal.

Forgiveness

It's nearly impossible to talk about family dysfunction and negative childhood experiences without raising the question of forgiveness. Questions, plural, is more like it. What is forgiveness, exactly? How might it help you? How do you forgive your parent, *if* you decide you want to?

You can find various concepts of forgiveness in the Bible, in psychotherapeutic literature, and in the media. It may be more helpful to discuss forgiveness in terms of what it isn't.

Forgiveness *does not* entail forgetting or denying your experiences. Forgiveness doesn't mean forgetting, minimizing, or denying the hurt you feel. It means acknowledging the wrongdoing, accepting the associated feelings, and letting go of holding the transgressions against the person responsible. It includes giving up the expectations you held and the beliefs that things should have been different. But no, you don't forget when you forgive. You simply reduce the hold the hurt has over you.

Forgiveness is not excusing or condoning. By forgiving someone, you're not sending a message that the person's behavior was acceptable or that you approve of it. For less significant infractions, you may be able to excuse or condone some things. Forgiveness is the big gun, called into play when you have been deeply harmed in some way. It may seem ironic, but it's those who have hurt you the most who may be the best candidates for your forgiveness.

Forgiveness is not a quick fix for an ailing relationship or a tool to use to avoid your own painful feelings about how you were treated. You may recall a time when a friend or relative said, "I'm not bitter anymore; I've forgiven so-and-so," when clearly they were still bubbling with anger and pain. Forgiveness is not a mantra to recite over and over in the hopes that one of these times you'll actually believe it. It's not a substitute for the difficult work of accepting and feeling painful emotions. Instead, think of it as a reward that you're able to bestow upon yourself afterward.

Forgiveness does not necessarily mean telling the people you've forgiven. You can tell them, should you choose, but in some cases the person you're forgiving may be long dead or not a part of your life anymore. That's fine. Forgiveness is something you do for you. No one else ever needs to know. You're under no obligation to inform.

Forgiveness does not entail expressions of remorse, regret, or contrition on the part of the person who hurt you. Some people decide that they won't forgive until the person in question has shown some indication of remorse or change, but forgiveness need not rely on anyone else's actions or intentions but your own. It's a unilateral decision—yours.

Forgiveness does not mean being the bigger person, being a martyr, doing the right thing. Again, you forgive for you, not because someone says you should.

Forgiveness is not a one time, one shot, all-or-nothing deal. Forgiveness isn't a single event, it's a process. You can forgive someone for certain deeds but not others. You can decide to forgive slowly, over the course of weeks, months, or years. You can change your mind about forgiveness, should your feelings change or new information come to light. You can even flat-out decide for now and forever that you don't want to forgive. It's up to you.

Beliefs about Forgiveness

We all hold certain beliefs about forgiveness, sayings that loop in our heads, messages we gleaned from grandparents, a teacher, spiritual advisors, friends. But they may not be accurate. Have you heard any of the following?

◊ Forgive and forget.

◊ Revenge is sweet.

◊ Just let it go.

◊ Forgiveness is for wimps, pushovers, and codependents; I stick to my guns.

◊ When you forgive, you're letting the other person off the hook.

◊ Forgiveness means I'll have to reconcile with the person, and there's no way I'm ready to do that.

◊ Now's your chance. If you don't forgive, you'll regret it when your mother/father is gone.

Are there others you've heard?

STOP AND THINK:
Forgiveness Myths and Beliefs

■ What are your own beliefs about forgiveness and where have they come from?

■ For those that seem like myths, write a new statement that changes the thought into a healthier one.

■ How do *you* define forgiveness? For example, you might start with, "Forgiveness is the process by which I . . .".

Why Forgive?

Valerie, forty-eight, chose to forgive her father because the depth of her anger was forcing her to "sink in the quicksand." After she forgave him, she noticed friends were commenting about "how good I looked and they wanted to know what I'd done."

Reasons to forgive include freeing yourself from being defined by the transgression or your painful, hurt feelings. This is in part what makes forgiveness so difficult. It may seem like if you forgive, you'll lose a part of yourself. In a way, you do. But it's a part that you may in fact be better off without since it harbors resentment, grudges, and ill will (sort of like an infected appendix that can burst and harm the rest of the body). Sure those feelings protect you from future hurt, but they also keep you tense and on guard, closed to others and to new experiences.

Forgiveness can help you find a sense of peace. With forgiveness, you acknowledge that you too are fallible, imperfect, and do the wrong thing sometimes. Forgiveness releases you from the spell of your own negative feelings. It helps you get on with your life. Your energy is no longer sapped by continued reactions to events of the past.

Are You Ready to Forgive?

Forgiveness sounds all well and good, but how do you know if you're ready? Valerie didn't think she was ready to forgive her father, but she happened to meet a follower of Buddhism and began chanting on a daily basis to relieve some of her anger. She began twice a day, chanting for as little as fifteen minutes to as long as forty-five minutes each time, closing her eyes, visualizing her father and wishing him happiness, health, and well-being. "The tears would gush almost every time," she says. During one chant, the idea of forgiveness came into her mind. "But I couldn't bring myself to say the words." After many more days of chanting, she was able to say them, and she visualized handing her father flowers. "Boy, did *that* bring the tears." But it also brought a feeling of peace that only increased with time.

To determine whether or not you're ready to forgive a parent, assuming you decide it's something you want to try, consider the questions that follow. And remember that there's no easy formula. These questions are just intended to prompt your exploration of the subject. Keep in mind that you don't have to forgive all at once—you can decide you'll forgive someone for certain things and not others, or that you'll forgive only one or two of the people who were involved in hurting or betraying you.

◊ Have you ever forgiven anyone in the past? What were the positive and negative consequences of your decision?

◊ Have you given yourself ample opportunity to *acknowledge, feel,* and *express* your hurt, anger, pain, whether to yourself, a friend, or therapist?

◊ Have you forgiven yourself first?

◊ Is your parent or the person you want to forgive ready to accept any responsibility? (In reality, this may be one of the things you set out to forgive—the person's unwillingness or inability to take ownership.)

◊ How will forgiveness help you? How will you feel as a result?

◊ What's your gut-level reaction to forgiveness?

◊ If you're not ready to forgive now, do you think you might be at some point?

There's no right way to forgive. Prayer, meditation, physical activity, sheer will, or writing (or any other form of creative expression) can help get you started. In addition to using one or more of these physical, emotional, spiritual, and creative outlets, write a list of who you want to forgive and, specifically, why. And remember that you can include your-self, as well as groups of people and systems (for example, a child welfare system that allowed you and your siblings to be separated and placed in foster homes, or a public assistance system that doesn't provide adequate psychological services for your parent with BPD). As you begin to develop an attitude of forgiveness, consider whether you want to do it silently or let others know, including perhaps the person you're forgiving. If you find you have trouble developing a forgiving attitude, that's fine too. Hurt is a big part of who we all are, and it may be difficult or impossible for you to forgive. It's better to acknowledge that you're not ready, even that you may never be, than to fake it. You will only deny your own feelings that way, which is the last thing you want to do!

CHAPTER 5

Overcoming Anger and Resentment

Anger. This powerful emotion tends to have negative connotations. But anger in and of itself isn't necessarily a bad thing. What's bad about anger are the actions you may impulsively take in response to it, as well as the long-term mental anguish you may feel as a result. Your goal in understanding anger shouldn't be to learn how never to be angry again. Anger is a legitimate feeling, one often designed for self-protection. And that feeling needs to be recognized and acknowledged just like all of your other emotions.

For adult children of a parent who may have been controlling, demanding, invalidating, or unaccepting of her child, it's common for anger to last a long time, perhaps years—and, for some, a lifetime. But although anger can be helpful in terms of self-preservation in the short term, it's not the best bet for your long-term well-being—physical, emotional, or social. This chapter will help you explore how you're using anger to protect yourself in some way from the hurt you experienced long ago and maybe even still from your parent today. It will also help you understand the different ways of coping with your anger, the toll it can take on you over time, and how to move beyond the chronic feelings you may be harboring.

Anger in Families

Anger, whether by its glaring presence or by its absence, plays a strong role in all families, but particularly in those where an adult shows border-line traits. In the *DSM-IV-TR* (2000), one of the criteria for the disorder is inappropriate, intense feelings of anger that are difficult for the person to control. But underexpression of anger may also be seen in those with BPD or borderline traits. According to Dr. Marsha Linehan, a borderline patient may also overcontrol angry feelings. "Many patients are afraid that if they do get angry, they will lose control and possibly react violently. They also fear that if they engage in hostile behavior, overtly or covertly, they will be rejected" (Linehan 1993a, p. 356). Given the intense fears of abandonment those with BPD feel, you can see why someone with the disorder might be fearful of expressing her anger.

Some adult children of parents with BPD recall their parent raging; screaming; beating them; storming out of the room, house, or car; threatening; throwing objects; name calling; and having tantrums. Others have trouble remembering any displays of anger in their homes. Instead, they may have experienced stony silences and heavy tension.

No Anger Allowed

Regardless of whether your parent overexpressed or underexpressed anger, she may not have accepted feelings of anger in you. "Go to your room until you can talk to me without being angry," or "How dare you be angry with me; I'm your mother/father," may have been said by a parent who was uneasy dealing with such feelings being directed at them. Or you may have heard, "What's wrong with you—why are you so angry?" or, "You must have PMS, you're really angry." Your parent couldn't accept that anger was an understandable response on your part, and that she might have been, in some part, its trigger.

"Anger was not an acceptable emotion in our house unless, of course, it was my mother who was ranting and raving and hurling dishes over some ridiculously inconsequential thing," says Melia, thirty-four. "We were taught to 'stifle it.' If we were angry, we'd get sent to our rooms, then punished, and sometimes beaten. As a result, I was so filled with rage, with no way of releasing the pressure, I thought I'd explode into a thousand pieces some day." She also recalls being humiliated pub-licly by her mother whenever she'd try to express anger. "She'd always find something to say, later on, in front of her friends, neighbors, or my friends that would embarrass me. Like she had to get even with me for disagreeing with her, like she had to break me. And she very nearly did."

Anger in a parent can be a terrifying thing for a child. Young children need to believe that their parent will protect them, that their parent is capable and right. If a parent is angry, therefore, the child believes it must be his fault, as the alternative is unthinkable. And he begins to suppress his own feelings, turning them inward rather than expressing them. Likewise, for the child who isn't allowed to be angry, whose anger is deflected by a parent (like a boomerang that comes hurtling back to you), a host of effects results, including feelings of guilt, depression, and chronic anger, all of which we'll discuss shortly.

What Is Anger?

Despite its bum rap from your borderline parent, the media, or society, anger is a normal emotion, one that's often designed to protect you when you've been scared or hurt. Anger can mobilize you against a pending physical attack (imagine the adrenaline rush and burst of energy you'd get upon the realization that a mugger were chasing you); it can tip you off that your boundaries have been encroached upon; it can help you get what you need.

Anger can also protect you from emotional pain. Imagine your partner of several years suddenly telling you he wants to end the relationship. You're devastated by the news. But your sadness and confusion quickly turn to rage. "How could he do this to me? After all I've invested in this relationship. Didn't I deserve to be told sooner? That asshole!"

Anger may be caused by feeling that you weren't validated, recognized, listened to, appreciated, or valued. It may be caused by feeling controlled—by another's will, expectations, demands, rules, or behavior—or that your boundaries were violated and your needs unmet. It's common for children to feel anger, for all of the reasons just stated, if their parents have trouble regulating their emotions and are self-involved and insecure.

For many people, it's easier—preferable—to feel anger rather than sadness, hurt, jealousy, shame, or other emotion. Anger compels you; there's energy in your anger, unlike with other emotions. And that energy gives you a sense of confidence that you can act to change your circumstances. Think of a time when you were saddened by something. Did you feel energized, driven to act? (More likely you felt tired, listless, driven only to the couch or to bed.)

How Anger Works

Although anger seems like a volatile, unpredictable emotion, its generation actually has a predictable cause-and-effect dynamic, as you can see from this formula we created, using concepts from *When Anger Hurts* (McKay, Rogers, and McKay 1989).

Antecedent Stress + Current Stress + Indirect Stressors + Trigger Thoughts = Anger

Antecedent stresses include your childhood experiences with your parent or other experiences you've stored away that influence your interpretation of current events.

Current stresses are painful emotions, unmet needs, or threats that you're experiencing in the present.

Think of indirect stressors as aggravating factors not directly related to the stimulus or current stress, but still influencing your reaction to it: extreme heat or cold, hunger or low-blood sugar, lack of sleep, hormonal fluctuations, pain, lack of physical activity, frustration, or overstimulation (too much noise, too large a crowd, and so on).

Add trigger thoughts, that is, cognitive sparks that act as a catalyst, to the mix and your stressors combine into a hostile affect (McKay, Rogers, and McKay 1989). Common trigger thoughts include the following:

◊ I don't deserve this.

◊ But that's not fair.

◊ You deliberately set out to hurt me.

◊ You knew better and you did it anyway.

◊ You're such a jerk.

Are there others you can think of?

What you do with anger is a choice, however. No, you can't remove antecedent stresses (though you can rethink how you interpret them), and you can't remove current stresses (though you can also rethink your interpretation of them). But how you fuel anger is a choice. You can minimize indirect stressors by taking care of yourself—eating when you need to eat, getting enough rest and exercise, removing yourself from taxing situations and learning how to manage them when you can't simply leave—and you can change your trigger thoughts so they don't ignite the waiting kindling.

STOP AND THINK: Reframing Triggers

In this exercise, based on concepts from McKay, Rogers, and McKay (1989), are several examples of how you can recast your trigger thoughts into beliefs that won't induce anger:

- "I don't deserve this" becomes "I'm free to want what I want, but others are under no obligation to provide it to me, particularly now that I'm an adult."

- "But that's not fair" becomes "Neither of our individual needs is more important than the other's. (There are few objective standards when it comes to fairness.)"

- "You deliberately set out to hurt me" becomes "Despite how appearances may seem, I really don't know all the motivations of others; I'm not a mind reader."

- "You knew better and you did it anyway" becomes "Knowing better doesn't mean others will necessarily do better; it all depends on what needs and motivations are the strongest at the time."

- "You're such a jerk" becomes "Labeling a person based on a particular action falsely implies that that's all there is to him or her, and that's rarely, if ever, the case."

What are some of your own trigger thoughts? Can you think of some ways to reframe them so that they no longer spark a blaze?

STOP AND THINK: Fiction and Fact

When it comes to anger, myths and beliefs abound. Which of the fictions below are your own? Which are widely accepted as truths by society?

- **When you get angry, it means you must be overreacting to something.**
  Fact. When you get angry, it may mean you're responding quite normally to a stimulus.

- **If I ignore my feelings of anger, they'll go away.**
  Fact. Like any other emotion, ignoring anger won't make it go away. Feelings need to be acknowledged, accepted, and worked through, unpleasant though it may be (at least for a while).

- **If I express my feelings of anger or irritation, it means I'm self-centered or difficult.**

Fact. Maybe some people will think you're self-centered and diffi-cult if you get angry, but that doesn't change the legitimacy of the emotion; it doesn't mean you should stifle it based on what some-one might think.

- **If a family member or friend makes me angry, I should just let it pass.**
  Fact. We'll discuss different ways to address anger later in this chapter; for now the shorter answer is that just letting it pass doesn't serve anyone well.

- **Revenge is sweet.**
  Fact. Vengefulness only leads to further resentment, and often—maybe even surprisingly—guilt.

- **Expressing anger is akin to losing control.**
  Fact. It depends on how you choose to express anger. Certainly, it's possible to lose control when sharing your feelings. Think of the person who starts screaming before he's tried to talk or the person who stomps out of a room and slams the door. That's los-ing control. But there are other ways to express anger, including writing or talking, that don't involve such extreme measures.

- **If the person who wronged me sees me so angry, she'll realize the effect she's having on me and change.**
  Fact. Don't count on it. People have to want to change. And they have to have the capacity to change. Thinking that your feelings can have so much influence is just setting yourself up for disap-pointment and hurt.

What are some other fictions you've heard about anger? Are there others besides those listed above?

Write a statement that changes the fictions into healthier facts.

The Many Faces of Anger

When you think of anger, you may envision someone yelling, screaming, threatening, and generally making a scene. But not everyone shows anger that way. Someone who is shy or inhibited might express her anger by withdrawing or being irritable. Someone who is laid-back in tem-perament might show his anger by not living up to a commitment he made.

Beth, thirty-five, was not a yeller. In fact, she prided herself on always remaining calm in confrontational situations with her borderline father. Whenever she was angry with him, she'd walk away and withdraw, then ruminate, first thinking critical thoughts about him and how he'd wronged her. Those critical thoughts would then center on her and her shortcomings—in not dealing with him effectively, in not being more understanding and compassionate of his diagnosis and his problems, in not being able to stand up to him like she'd wanted to for years. When her therapist asked her one day whether she thought she was angry, harboring resentment, she was astonished. "No, the last thing I am is an *angry* person." But as her therapist pointed out, she was indeed angry, and it had been simmering for years, since from the time she was quite young, Beth was taught that good girls don't raise their voices or "talk back" to their parents. She'd never been allowed to express her anger, and so it presented itself, as her therapist noticed, in frequent and damaging critical thoughts.

Anger can be expressed in many, seemingly surprising, ways. As you read the following list, see if you recognize any of these expressions of chronic anger in yourself:

- ◊ bitterness
- ◊ comparing yourself to others and feeling that they have it easier than you do
- ◊ critical thoughts, about others as well as yourself
- ◊ feeling inwardly annoyed and frustrated when someone doesn't understand you
- ◊ thinking of your rebuttal when someone is trying to talk with you, acting defensively
- ◊ guilt
- ◊ impatience
- ◊ muscle tension
- ◊ difficulty letting go of past resentments
- ◊ difficulty listening and taking someone else's viewpoint into account
- ◊ persistently feeling life isn't fair
- ◊ sarcasm
- ◊ dread

◊ irritation

◊ shutting down when upset with someone

◊ speaking insensitively to others, perhaps feeling guilty about it afterward (or not)

◊ an attitude of "whatever," or "so what—I don't really care."

STOP AND THINK: What Anger Looks Like

Write down the names of three to five people who are close to you.

Think about an incident or two when you got angry with each of them. Try to remember what the antecedent stresses, current and indirect stressors, and your trigger thoughts were.

How did you express your anger toward each person? Did you respond in any of the ways listed above? Do you see any patterns in your responses? Did your expressions differ with each person, for instance, "My mother—I usually end up snapping at her. I say something like, 'We have to end this conversation,' and I hang up. Once some time passes, I feel so guilty, I call her back. The whole time, I realized just recently, my jaw and hands are clenched and my stomach hurts."

Now go back and consider each of the stressors and trigger thoughts. How might you reframe them to lessen your anger response?

Coping Styles

While expressions of anger may have infinite variety, they usually rely on one of five coping styles: denial, passive, aggressive, passive aggressive, assertive.

Denial

Someone who denies his anger may think things such as, "I'm not really angry, I'm just a little upset right now. But it will pass." Coping with anger by suppressing it, however, leads to growing feelings of resentment and even physical ailments like headaches, stomachaches, and sleep problems, since the anger is turned inward rather than acknowledged and expressed. Sometimes a person denies their own feelings and projects them onto someone else. For example, they may say (in an angry tone), "I'm not angry; you are."

Passive

Those who cope with anger passively shy away from any sort of conflict, so fearful are they of upsetting or offending others. They have a hard time saying no, so they tend to end up obliging others halfheartedly but with a smile, then feeling helpless and frustrated inside.

Aggressive

Those who cope with their anger aggressively want to make others pay for their misdeeds, or perceived misdeeds. They want to blame and punish, and they don't shrink from doing it in an in-your-face manner. People on the receiving end feel intimidated, threatened, defensive, and they soon learn to be on guard against the person who expresses anger aggressively.

Passive-Aggressive

Someone who responds to anger passively holds in their anger and feels frustrated as a result. That sense of frustration builds to a critical threshold, where the next trigger ignites an outburst, though it still doesn't address the underlying or original issue (McKay, Rogers, and McKay 1989). Another example of the passive-aggressive coping mechanism is the person who smiles and says, "No, really. I'm not angry about the situation." A couple of days later, when his wife asks him to fix her closet door, he says he will. Two weeks later, it's still not done.

Assertive

Anger expressed assertively, that is directly, takes into account the needs of all parties involved. It involves communicating facts and feelings along with a request for a change in behavior. It removes judgment, assumptions, and blame. In chapter 6, we'll discuss how specifically to use the assertive coping style with your borderline parent (or others in your life as well). To fully overcome any suppressed or long-term anger you've been letting brew, adding this style of expression to your emotional and communication repertoire is critical.

Most people have more than one style of expressing their anger depending on the situation, the history, the person or people involved, and their own present physical and mental state.

For each coping style, try to think of a situation where you would express your anger in that way.

Once you've done that, reflect on which style you use the most, which you use the least, not at all. Which seems most effective to you? Why?

Who Would You Be without Your Anger?

Whatever your typical coping style (and you may find that you don't adhere to just one style, but rather employ elements of each, depending on the circumstances), the thought of letting go of chronic anger can be a frightening one. "My anger was like a combination jet-propulsion backpack and security blanket that I kept on me all the time," says Caitlin, the daughter of a woman with BPD who would rage violently but threaten to put her daughter out on the street if she dared to express her angry feelings. "It drove me, and it made me feel secure. I knew that with it on, no one would ever treat me the way my mother did." But the downside of Caitlin's anger was that she was always on alert against a pending attack. She'd shoot back quickly, making defensive remarks when friends would make a benign comment. Then she'd feel bad afterward for having misinterpreted what they'd meant—so bad that it became easier just to minimize contact. She withdrew, kept herself busy with schoolwork, and felt increasingly lonely.

With the help of her therapist, Caitlin realized that the root of her loneliness and distance from others was because of the anger she was carrying around. "But I was afraid if I started to let it out, to unpack the backpack, that I'd never be able to stop."

But Who Are You with Your Anger?

Scary as it is to face feelings of chronic anger, keeping them carefully stowed away doesn't serve you well either. Consider the expense: Anger causes the body to release hormones that, over time, damage nearly all systems of your body. Those hormones have been implicated in causing or exacerbating numerous physical conditions, everything from autoimmune disorders to heart disease and hypertension.

Emotionally, chronic anger can affect your sense of well-being, self-esteem, and your relationships. It can lead to withdrawal, isolation and loneliness, hypersensitivity, being closed and suspicious (ready to pounce at any stimulus that may remotely resemble a past offense), depression, and self-destructive behaviors such as overeating, drug or alcohol abuse, and even suicide attempts.

STOP AND THINK: Anger's Consequences

In what ways has chronic anger affected your life? This exercise, adapted from McKay, Rogers, and McKay (1989) will help you look at some of the consequences of anger. On a scale of 1 to 5, one being "very little," and 5 indicating "a great deal," assess the impact anger has had on each of the areas that follow:

_____ how you get along with bosses at work

_____ how you interact with coworkers

_____ your relationships with subordinates

_____ the first impression you make upon meeting new people

_____ how you treat your children

_____ your relationship with your romantic partner

_____ former relationships with friends and partners

_____ how you get along with your neighbors

_____ how you interact with volunteer organizations you're part of, or recreational groups, religious organizations

_____ lost relationships and estrangements

_____ your physical health

_____ your emotional health

_____ any drinking or drug use you engage in

_____ unsafe sexual practices you engage in

_____ your sense of creativity

_____ how productive you are

_____ your driving

_____ your accuracy, retention, and memory

Any area where you responded with a 2 or higher may be an area you may to work on. Continue reading. We'll talk about how to minimize the effects of anger shortly.

Keeping Tabs on Your Anger

Designate a section of your journal to keep track of your anger as you continue to work through this chapter, the remainder of the book, and beyond. This will help you see the changes in the level of your chronic anger as well as the decreasing impact it has on your life and health over time.

Write in your journal at least once each day. Set aside a time to do this, for example, first thing in the morning, after dinner or before bed. Be careful not to let other obligations interfere with this time. Note the following:

◊ The number of times you felt angry over the past twenty-four hours and the cause or trigger.

◊ Following each, rate your level of arousal or intensity of feeling on a scale from 1 to 10, using physiological responses as a guide (for example, racing heart, chest tightening, headache); a 1 indicates "minimal arousal," and 10 indicates "the most I've ever felt."

◊ What urge accompanied each and, using the same scale, how strong was that urge?

◊ Finally, how did you respond? Rate the level of any aggressive response (including behaviors) on a scale from 1 to 10 and what that response was: 1 indicates "minimal aggression," and 10, "the most I've ever displayed."

Here's an example of what a journal entry would look like:

November 22   3 times.

> 1. *When my child wouldn't get dressed for school and we missed the bus as a result.*
> Arousal: 7
> Urge: 9 (*I wanted to drag her in her pajamas to the bus stop.*)

Aggressive response: 6 (*I yelled at her, told her she'd have conse-quences to deal with later and didn't kiss her goodbye when she got out of the car.*)

2. *When I vented to my mother on the phone later in the day and she told me she thought it was "just desserts" that I had a daughter as difficult as I was.*
Arousal: 7
Urge: 10 (*I wanted to yell, "I can't believe what a bitch you are."*)
Aggressive response: 2 (*I said, "Mom, there's someone at the door. I need to go now," and I hung up.*)

3. *When my husband told me "it wasn't too bright" for me to have told my mother about what happened with my daughter this morning.*
Arousal: 5
Urge: 5 (*I wanted to hit him.*)
Aggressive response: 9 (*I lost it with him. How dare he side with my mother. I screamed, slammed the door, threw his work files at him, and pushed him away when he tried to talk to me about it.*)

Over time, you'll start to discern patterns in who and what triggers your anger, as well as why and how you respond with different coping styles to different people. In the example above, this woman may have a tendency to get angry when she feels that her needs (to get her daughter to the bus on time) and feelings (of frustration) aren't taken seriously. In response, she seems to employ an aggressive style with her daughter and husband but a passive style with her mother. Over time, it can be useful to look at how you rate the intensity of your anger. As you continue to work on your responses, you may begin to see a decrease in the intensity.

For an additional challenge, as you keep tabs on your anger, identify the stressors and trigger thoughts that contributed to feeling angry. Then reframe the thought. For example, your journal entry may look like this:

1. *When my child wouldn't get dressed for school and we missed the bus as a result.*
Antecedent stressor: *My mother was often depressed and so she rarely got up to help us get dressed or cook us breakfast. When she did, it was obvious she'd rather be doing anything but that.*
Current stressor: *We all overslept. My daughter woke up on the wrong side of the bed and was uncooperative.*
Indirect stressors: *I woke up with a headache, and if she missed the bus, this would be the third time in two weeks that I'd be late*

for work.

Trigger thoughts: *She knows that if she doesn't get herself dressed on time, I end up being late. She's selfish.*

Reframed trigger thoughts: *She's a child. She was having a slow morning, and her need to take her time overrode any concern that her dawdling might affect me. She's not selfish; she was acting like a normal child who wasn't quite ready to go off to school when I needed to leave.*

Doing a Body Scan

For the first two weeks of keeping your anger journal, it will also be useful to note where in your body you really feel the anger. You can do this by *scanning* your body, a technique that's often used in yoga, meditation, and biofeedback to locate areas where you hold on to stress, tightness, and tension.

Be sure you'll have a few minutes that are free of interruptions to do the following exercise, adapted from McKay, Rogers, and McKay (1989).

1. Sit or lie down so you're comfortable. Pay attention to your feet and legs. Wiggle your toes, then rotate your feet and relax them. Note any tension in your calves. Let go of it if it's there.

2. Focus on your lower torso. Do you feel any tension or pain in your lower back? Relax and take a deep breath. Notice any tension in your hips, pelvic area, or buttocks. Consciously relax those areas.

3. Now focus on your diaphragm and stomach. Take two or three slow, deep breaths. Feel yourself relaxing, and note any tension you still feel in this area.

4. Note your lungs and chest cavity. Is there tension there? Take a couple of deep breaths and envision the air filling these areas. Relax more deeply.

5. Key into your shoulders, neck, and throat. Swallow a couple of times and notice any tension or soreness in your throat and neck. Roll your head clockwise, then counterclockwise. Shrug your shoulders and notice any tension. Relax.

6. Starting at the top of your head, notice any tension or pain. Scan down to your forehead and relax it. Note any tension behind

your eyes, your ears, in your cheeks, in your jaw. Relax your mouth, lips, tongue, and chin.

7. Go back and scan your body for any remaining tension. Breathe deeply and relax.

8. Note in your journal where you were holding tension.

Finding the Source

As with other emotions, in order to halt their negative effects, you must first understand where they originated. As stated earlier, adult children of a parent with BPD may have chronic feelings of anger for a variety of reasons, encompassing everything from repeated invalidation to physical assaults to trying to address issues of contention with the parent and encountering hostility, denial, or projection.

STOP AND THINK: From the Source

What are the issues that are causing your feelings of anger? List them in your journal. They can be as detailed or as generic as you want. Don't censor yourself; there are no standards for what are legitimate reasons for your feelings. Examples might include "I tried hard to be good, but my parent always found something to criticize"; "I'm angry because I wasn't allowed to express my feelings growing up; I felt stifled"; or, "You didn't take care of me the way I needed you to. You put me in situations that forced me to accept adult responsibilities and endangered me, like leaving me with Uncle Martin when you were off with your boyfriend and he abused me sexually."

For each item, how have you expressed your anger about it (consider your coping style, your level of arousal and aggression)? Have you written about it, addressed it with the person involved, acted in such a way that you felt guilty for later? What were the results and consequences?

What would you like to do to be able to let go of some of those feelings now, to minimize their intensity and effects?

Strategies for Reducing Anger

Keeping your anger journal, noticing the patterns that emerge, and revisiting the exercises in this chapter periodically will help you begin to reduce your anger. There are also many things you can incorporate into your life that will reduce feelings of chronic anger. Here are a few to start with, and there's space for you to add your own at the end of the list. Do these as often as you want or need to.

- deep breathing (slow, deep breaths with inhalations and exhalations of similar duration and a pause between them)

- visualization or guided imagery (of calming places, people you enjoy being around, and so on—don't replay unpleasant or angry scenes)

- prayer or meditation

- yoga, tai chi, Pilates

- doing volunteer work or just helping a friend with a chore now and then

- writing down how you feel, and how you want to feel

- engaging in other creative arts

- doing any aerobic exercise (walking, running, swimming, biking, skiing, skating, kick boxing)

- screaming into a pillow or in the car

- beating a pillow, punching a punching bag

- tearing up sheets of newspaper

-

-

-

-

As you can see, some of these strategies are ways of venting or expressing anger, while others distract you from it—some get you more in touch with your feelings, and some help you distance them. It's important to find a balance between the two. Always distracting yourself from your anger means that it will come up in inappropriate ways at inappropriate times, toward people in your life who did nothing to deserve it. Likewise, always venting your anger means you relive it again and again, never giving yourself a mental break from it. You might consider using a mental image to help you find the right balance. You might try visualizing a metronome, a pendulum on a clock, a seesaw, or a balance scale.

CHAPTER 6

Communicating and Setting Limits

You may still feel resentment from your past, and when interacting with your parent today, those old feelings may be quickly triggered and exacerbated. This chapter offers several concepts and communication tools you can explore that will further reduce the stress and strain and volatility of your present dealings with a difficult parent.

At times your feelings of frustration, of being trapped, of helplessness, may seem overwhelming. But you can set limits and communicate them to your parent, and express your feelings more directly and effectively, thereby changing the interaction. The end result? Your sense of control will increase. You will stand up for yourself in a way that honors who you are and what you believe and is also respectful of your parent. You will no longer play the role you were assigned as a child and, perhaps still, as an adult. Old, unhealthy dynamics will change.

Finding the Right Balance

For some adult children, not having any involvement with a parent is the easiest answer. They may not know exactly how to set limits with their parent, or their limits may be continually tested and breached. They find it easier to sever ties.

Others, regardless of past wrongs and abuse, find a way to navigate a relationship in the present that meets at least some of their (and their parent's) needs. Some interact with their parent, but on a superficial level. "My father and I are like anchors on TV news," says Talia, twenty-two. "We speak in not much more than sound bites, covering the news, weather, and sports. Anything other than that usually ends up in a fight." Others, whether out of guilt, obligation, fear, or another need, maintain a relationship in which past abuse continues.

There's no right or wrong choice in how you choose to deal with your parent, now that you're an adult. What's important is that you make your own thoughtful, deliberate choices that respect and protect yourself, and if you're a parent, your minor children.

The decision about your level of involvement with your parent isn't a static one; it can change over time as circumstances, your needs, and your parent's control over his emotions and actions all shift. You may decide to distance yourself for a few months, only answering occasional light emails from your parent but not communicating by phone or in person, while you gather your thoughts and do some soul-searching about your true feelings, for instance. Or perhaps because of a move closer to where your parent lives, you find yourself in contact more than ever before. You may decide to really put the tools in this chapter into practice and notice that your relationship improves and your stress level decreases. Or you may find that the increased interaction is just too draining, and despite living closer, you only talk on the phone and visit once a year. Once again, the choice is yours now.

STOP AND THINK: Meeting Needs

To help you think more about your comfort level with interaction, consider what needs the relationship is meeting *for you*. Here are some examples:

- She's my mother, and I can't stand the thought of just walking away from such an important relationship.

- It's easier to let my controlling mother make decisions for me, than for me to make them myself.

- I have to admit, I get a burst of energy—like a rush—after we fight.

- When he's not acting bizarrely, he's really a great person to be around; he's funny and engaging, and my kids love hearing the stories from his childhood.

Fear can make you stay in a relationship without addressing significant issues with another person. When you think about confronting your parent with the relationship issues that trouble you, do you feel afraid? If so, try to identify what you fear. Some examples include:

- I'm afraid I'll lose his approval. I only feel loved and valued when I go along with him. I know that.

- If I were to confront her, she'd probably threaten to do something. Who knows what she'd end up doing?

- I can't bear another one of those rages. I just keep my mouth shut and it's fine.

- I'm afraid I'd feel so guilty if I upset her. She already has such a hard time with things, how can I in good conscience add to the load?

- He might start drinking again. Then how would I feel?

Controlling the Flow

As you work through this chapter, keep in mind that there are many ways for you to control the flow of communication. Keep in mind that you have the *right* to do this. The following are just a few ideas. Spend some time thinking of others that will work specifically for you, given your own preferences and circumstances.

- ◊ Screen phone calls with answering machines, voicemail, and caller ID, so you can answer only those you feel up to taking.

- ◊ Block, filter, and/or delete e-mail.

- ◊ Ask your partner to say you're unavailable at the moment and you'll return the call when you can.

- ◊ If you're in the same space as your parent, you can leave the room or leave the house, put on headphones, turn on the television, pick up your knitting project, or go outside to do some gardening.

- ◊ You can say you're not prepared to discuss particular issues right now and suggest a better time.

- ◊ Refuse packages; don't open mail; return mail to sender.

- ◊ Change telephone numbers; get an unlisted phone number.

◊ Make sure no one other than the residents of your home has access to it (keys, lock combinations, garage door openers, alarm codes, and so on).

◊ During visits with your parent, stay in motels, hotels, or with friends in the area. When your parent comes to visit, insist that he do the same.

Keep Your Eye on the Prize

Maintaining a relationship, to whatever degree you choose, if any, doesn't mean denying that you have—and hopefully are working through—past resentments, or denying the fact that you're still set off by things your parent says and does today. Try thinking of it instead as moving forward while you revise troublesome scripts. Keep in mind that you can't expect your parent to change, but you can change *your* attitudes, interpretations, your responses, thereby modifying the dynamics.

Imagine that you and your parent are dancing a waltz together, with your parent leading. You've always waltzed with him. Come to think of it, you've never liked the waltz. So you signal to the orchestra to play a tango, and you begin to lead. It's going to be nearly impossible for your parent to continue that waltz while you're doing the tango. He may not like the tango. He may storm off the dance floor. He may scream that you are selfish and would do anything, stooping so low as to conspire with the musicians, to prevent his happiness. But he's also likely to realize at some point that if he wants to dance with you, he'll need to change his steps.

You may notice that asserting your boundaries and communicating more directly with your parent actually makes life more difficult at first. Keep your eye on what you hope to gain, however, and remember that squelching discussion of difficult issues because you know they'll meet with a bad reaction only deepens your anger and makes it harder for you to relate to the other person. It may not be the best choice for either one of you.

STOP AND THINK: Now or Later

To weigh the short-term versus long-term effects of asserting your limits with your parent, think of a particular issue that's been a cause of contention in the past. Write it down in your journal.

By way of example, Bethany doesn't want to spend Thanksgiving with her mother and stepfather this year. She says that one too many celebrations have been overshadowed by her stepfather's characteristic grandiosity and her mother's martyrdom. She can't bear another painfully detailed recounting of how much work went into the lavish spread they insisted on preparing. But she knows that breaking the news to her mother will entail a lecture on how selfish she is, coupled with a temper tantrum and a tense silence for weeks to follow. Of course, her sister will call too and start in on her for hurting Mom. Bethany thinks maybe she should just go this year and put off making a change until next year. She's said this for the past three years.

Have you, like Bethany, been putting off addressing an issue because you're afraid of the results? Make a chart with two columns, one labeled "now," the other "later." Draw two rows underneath the columns and label one row "positives" and the other row "negatives." Now, looking at your own issue, what do you think you might gain by confronting your parent now? What might you gain by waiting? Write your answers under "positives," "now" and "later," respectively.

Now write down the negatives. What are the downsides of confronting your parent now? What are the downsides of waiting?

For Bethany, if she confronts her mother now, she's likely to feel a sense of relief and to enjoy a quiet holiday at home with her husband, her kids, and some friends. She will have broken a pattern and she'll have an easier time making and communicating her decision in the years to come. If she waits, she's likely to feel temporary relief—until next year rolls around. She can also find some middle ground, perhaps going for just one night instead of the usual week-long trip.

Now consider the negatives for Bethany. If she addresses the issue now, Bethany will have to deal with her mother's tantrum and silence, and grief from her sister. If she waits to have the discussion, she'll have to suffer through an unpleasant dinner when she'd really rather be at home; she'll feel the same sense of dread as next Thanksgiving gets closer; and she'll feel like a wimp for not speaking up.

What do your answers tell you about your own difficult issue? They may not provide a clear-cut solution, and they may not take away that feeling in the pit of your stomach as you think about talking to your parent. But your answers will help you identify your feelings, needs, and priorities.

Remember that you're charting new territory in the relationship, and the road ahead is not a smooth one. Think of your project as clearing a path through a jungle with only a machete. Sure, over time you'll do it, but not without mosquito bites, calloused hands, nicks and cuts, some moments of extreme frustration, and the knowledge that some or much of the greenery you cleared will grow back and will need to be cleared again. (Next time, though, it will be easier since the roots aren't as firmly entrenched and it hasn't been growing for as long.)

Try to identify the direction in which you see your relationship with your parent heading. What are your goals for the relationship? Since you can't expect him or her to change, what's realistic? Examples of goals include the following:

- I want to have a relationship where I'm not always reacting to my mother's crises and dropping everything to go help her.

- I really want to stop feeling like a scared little girl again every time she gets angry with me.

- My goal is to maintain a relationship with my father but not let him interfere with my marriage.

- It's really important to me that my kids get to know their grand-mother, but other than supervising to protect them, I need to stay removed as much as possible.

- Right now, I just can't think about any relationship with my parent.

Know Your Rights

In any relationship, you have rights. Because someone is your parent or has significant emotional challenges doesn't change your right to your rights! You'll want to keep this list in mind as you read further and find your equilibrium in the relationship. You have the right

- ◊ to feel safe in the relationship

- ◊ to be treated respectfully

- ◊ to not be abused verbally, emotionally, or physically

- ◊ to be heard

- ◊ to be appreciated and valued

- ◊ to have your privacy and boundaries respected

- ◊ to have your needs met

- ◊ to feel good about yourself in the relationship

STOP AND THINK: Relationship Rights

The previous list is not fixed. Can you think of other rights? What does each right mean to you? For instance, "to feel safe in the relationship" might mean not worrying that at any moment your parent may let loose with a torrent of criticism at you.

Tools and Techniques for Gaining Control

The remainder of this chapter contains a series of exercises, questions, and tools for you to use to minimize angry reactions to things your parent says and does, to confront and diffuse difficult situations, and to express your emotions more directly. You can use these guidelines to deal with a wide variety of issues, from handling challenging family events such as birthdays, holidays, funerals, and weddings (times when abandonment fears and other emotions may run particularly high in those with borderline traits), for instance, to explaining that you can no longer provide the financial support you once did to your parent. You can apply them to relatively minor, mundane issues as well as major conflicts. And you can use them in other areas of your life and with other people as well.

Bring Awareness to the Table

Remember what you learned when you were taught to cross the street? Stop, look, and listen. The same principles help in other situations. Before and during any contact with your parent, or other difficult individual, it's important to be mindful of how you feel. Often, particularly when you're under stress, it may be hard to really know. Perhaps, even more often, you may just not stop to think about it.

Start noticing your own cues instead of overlooking them. What physical sensations do you feel? Common physical reactions to anger include pounding temples; "seeing white," or light; a feeling of vibration in the head; ringing in your ears; flushing in the cheeks; clenched jaws and fists; muscle tension in the arms, legs, neck, and shoulders; rapid, shallow breathing; the feeling of burning or a knot in the stomach; and nausea.

Note whether and how your stance and posture change. Do you suddenly feel more comfortable with your arms crossed in front of you, protectively? Do you tense your shoulders and round your back, symbolically protecting your chest? Do you stiffen and change your position to one where you're ready to make an escape from the situation? For example, if you were sitting, do you stand up and face the direction of the doorway, now that you're feeling threatened? It may be helpful to use the body scan exercise from chapter 5 to help you detect where in your body you're reacting.

What other emotions do you feel? Are you scared? Sad? Hurt? What emotions do you anticipate having after the interaction? For example, after you get angry and have words with your parent, does guilt inevitably follow for you?

What thoughts are you having? What are some of those continuous-loop messages that you hear in your head?

Notice what effects you anticipate as a result of your contact. Do you sense you'll be too wiped out and drained to go to work the next day or to give your toddler a bath later in the evening?

Ease Up on the Judgment

Recognizing and accepting how you feel is the first step toward working through it. You can't change what you don't acknowledge. You may not like that you have certain feelings about your parent and your relationship. You may not like that you shake with anxiety before going to visit your father, but—obvious and trite as it may sound—that's where you are right now. So regardless of how you *feel* about how you feel, don't censor or judge yourself.

STOP AND THINK: How Judgmental Are You?

On a scale from 1 to 5, 1 indicating that you don't agree at all and 5 indicating that you agree entirely, rate how closely you identify with each of the following statements:

1. I wish I didn't get so worked up every time I think about talking to my mother.

2. I really shouldn't have such guilty feelings.

3. I should be calmer and less afraid whenever I get ready to visit my parents.

4. I hate myself for being so angry at him.

5. I'm a lousy son for feeling like this about my mother.

Now add up your ratings. The higher your score, the more you're judging your feelings in a way that may be hampering your ability to change them; learning to take a nonjudgmental stance toward your own emotions should be a priority as you continue to read this chapter and book.

For every statement above for which you responded with a 3, a 4, or a 5, recast it into something less judgmental. For example, "I really shouldn't have such guilty feelings" can be recast to, "Now that I realize how guilty I feel, I can work to understand why and lessen those feelings so they're not as overwhelming," or "Like it or not, right now that's just the way I feel."

Out, Out, Damned Triggers

As we discussed, triggers are those emotional sparks that ignite anger and other emotions. It's important for you to know what yours are. In dealing with your parent, there are likely behaviors and/or words that set you off, not because they're so terrible in and of themselves, done or said *in isolation*, but because you're experiencing them in context—that is, through your past experience and your present emotions. Once you recognize your triggers, you can do something about them.

Actions Speak Loudly

It may seem like there's a huge list of things your parent does that make you see red. If you think about it though, it's likely that they fall into categories; that is, the particular circumstances may be different each time, but the core trigger is the same. Here are some examples:

Violating boundaries. Michelle's mother frequently drops by without calling first to see if it's okay. Sometimes she'll bring candy for Michelle's children, which Michelle has repeatedly told her not to do. On a couple of occasions when Michelle was out, she cleaned her kitchen and left a note about what bad shape it had been in.

Not respecting privacy. Michelle has also caught her mother, on more than one occasion, rifling through Michelle's husband's drawers looking for money she's convinced he has stashed.

STOP AND THINK: Know Your Action Triggers

What are your triggers? In addition to the behaviors that trigger you, try to describe how your anger plays out, the specific circumstances.

What messages do these incidents send to you each time they occur? Imagine you had never laid eyes on your parent before—you two are perfect strangers—and she did something that you've identified as a trigger. What would you think then? Would you get angry? How would you respond?

Words Speak Loudly Too

Triggers can also be verbal. Do you take a deep breath and tense up each time you hear the word "always" come out of your father's mouth? Does the phrase, "If only you'd been . . ." give you a migraine? Words and phrases that may trigger anger include:

- ◊ "You always . . .".
- ◊ "You never . . .".
- ◊ "You're so . . .".
- ◊ "You don't . . .".
- ◊ "You should . . .".
- ◊ "Someday maybe you'll be able to understand . . .".

Other verbal triggers may include:

Accusations, criticism, or personal attacks. Don's mother, without fail, comments sarcastically on his wife's parenting methods at family get-togethers. She also harps on him about his weight.

Blaming. Whenever Michelle tries to talk to her mother about her out-of-control spending habits, her mother blames Michelle's father for not leaving more money to his estate when he died.

Projecting. Michelle's mother repeatedly tells Michelle that (on top of being a poor housekeeper and mother) she really ought to learn how to manage her money. Really, it's Michelle's mother that needs some money-management tips.

Other triggers may include your parent asking for help (or the way he asks for help); invalidation of your opinions, feelings, and expressed wishes; black-and-white thinking; teasing; rehashing the past; and self-pity.

STOP AND THINK: Know Your Verbal Triggers

What are your verbal triggers? Are there others in addition to those listed here?

What do your verbal triggers say to you? For instance, when your parent says, "If only you'd been more like your sister," you might interpret it as, "I love you less than her. I don't value who you are."

Imagine you had never laid eyes on your parent before—you two are perfect strangers—and he made one of the statements you've identified as a trigger. What would you hear then? Would you get angry? How would you respond?

Context Is Key

As with just about all aspects of life, context is everything. If your house is spotless, and your mother says you're a lousy housekeeper, well, it's pretty easy to feel confident she's mistaken. You're more likely to write off the comment as another instance of her projection. But if your house is messy one day and she says the same thing, then you might be annoyed at her criticism.

Similarly, you may notice that you're more quick to get angry in certain circumstances or settings than others. Maybe when your parents are at your home, you tend to let things go more easily, but if you're visiting them in their home, you have less control and feel overwhelmed by what they do or say. Or maybe you can handle phone conversations easily, but reading your mother's long, rambling e-mails makes you grit your teeth. Perhaps when others are around, your parent demonstrates nothing but adoration and respect for you, but as soon as you're alone, the accusations start flying. Or vice versa. Competing with others for your time and attention may be what brings on borderline behavior, so you find you'd rather interact with your parent one-on-one.

STOP AND THINK:
Know Your Contextual Triggers

What are your contextual triggers? Do you notice patterns to how, when, or where you're the most likely to be triggered? Does it happen on certain holidays? With certain relatives present? In particular places or circumstances? Note your contextual triggers in your journal.

For each trigger, brainstorm a way to minimize or eliminate it. For instance, if you tend to feel angry around your parents because of how they play off each other and take sides against you when you're all together, you can commit to meeting with them by themselves. You can meet your mother for breakfast, and invite your father over for lunch.

You Aren't Made of Steel

Being human, you have your moments—or days or weeks!—of weakness. Factors that may make it harder to manage your triggers and resulting emotions may include not getting enough sleep (fatigue), physical illness or chronic pain, financial worries, relationship concerns, work demands, anxiety about particular situations, substance use, side effects from prescription medications, lack of physical activity, and numerous other things.

While you can't always control every single thing that increases your chances of having negative feelings triggered, knowing what your vulnerabilities are helps you work *with* them, rather than be ruled by them. If you know you're at your wit's end every Thursday because you have a standing deadline at work on Fridays, Thursday night probably isn't the best time to have dinner with your father. Likewise, if you're completing a course of radiation therapy, you might want to wait a few weeks to take that trip to see your mother. Knowing what your sore spots are helps you to minimize their impact, and it helps you assert yourself in situations where you likely feel overwhelmed or out of control.

It's not easy to admit to being human. Accept that you'll be more vulnerable at certain times than others. Don't beat yourself up.

STOP AND THINK:
Know What Makes You React

What makes you more vulnerable to your triggers? Make sure as you write them in your journal that you use judgment-free statements to describe them. Just stick to the facts. For example, "When I don't get nine hours of sleep, I'm irritable and anxious the next day," or "When my arthritis flares, it's hard for me to have the patience to listen to my mother's rants."

For each one, try to think of ways you can minimize its effects in terms of dealing with your parent: "When I have plans to visit my father, I know I need to get some extra sleep the night before. If I can't for some reason, I'll call him in the morning and reschedule or I'll make sure I can get in an hour of yoga before I leave home. That will help alleviate some of the irritability and anxiety."

Difficult Parents Are People Too

Just as you have triggers of all sorts and vulnerabilities, so too does your parent. In fact, someone who has difficulty handling his or her emotions and has a heightened sensitivity to emotional stimuli may feel as though just about everything in life is a trigger.

While you have to focus on your own well-being, it can be helpful to note what your parent's triggers and weak spots are as well. No, you don't want to concentrate all of your time, energy, and attention on your parent and her needs (you may very well feel that you've already done enough of this throughout your life, thank you very much), but being aware of what sets your parent off—to the extent that it's predictable— will ultimately help you.

Common triggers for someone with BPD or its traits are

◊ threats of abandonment, perceived in things as seemingly minor as you saying you have to get off the phone in a few minutes or that you can't come over tomorrow night because you have theater tickets

◊ an intolerance of being alone, physically or emotionally

◊ feeling misunderstood

◊ having a request denied

◊ stress

◊ uncertainty or change

◊ experiencing a *perceived* loss (of status, money, a relationship, attention, loyalty)

◊ medication, nonprescription substances, and other environmental stimuli.

STOP AND THINK:
Know Your Parent's Triggers

- What are the behavioral, verbal, and contextual triggers you've noticed for your parent?

- What seem to be his/her weaknesses?

- Are there ways you can work around them? If so, how might you modify your communication and interaction to do so?

Know Your Priorities

Though you may not consciously realize it, in every interaction you have (with anyone), you have priorities. No, it's not as devious as it sounds, but you do have an agenda of sorts when you communicate with others. For instance, you may be focused on expressing an opinion, saying no, asking for a favor, offering help, or increasing the closeness of a relationship. And your agenda dictates the words you choose, the tone of your voice, even your body language.

Your agenda may change from interaction to interaction. For instance, at one point in time, it may be most important to you to communicate your dissatisfaction with your parent's unwillingness to accept responsibility for a drinking problem. With your next conversation, you may decide that you won't be satisfied until you've come to mutual undertstanding about an issue and can end the conversation with "I love you," the way you used to.

STOP AND THINK:
Know Your Goals

Think of a recent or upcoming interaction with your parent. Describe the situation as completely as possible. What makes it a troubling situation?

Now think about what results you want to see. How do you want to feel about yourself and your relationship afterward? How do you hope your parent will feel?

Which results are the most important to you in this particular interaction?

Note: It may be difficult to clearly rank your desired outcomes. Rather than providing definitive answers, going through this process will help you better understand your own needs and how they translate into the choices you make about communication—when, where, how.

Communicating as Clearly as a Bell

The suggestions below can be incorporated into conversations about a wide range of circumstances, from the ordinary and everyday to the serious. They're meant to help you express your needs in a way that's respectful of your parent—or anyone else with whom you use them. You'll want to adapt them to your own personal style, using words and sequences that are comfortable. And you'll want to practice. Try some of them out on the next telemarketer who calls, or a store clerk or customer service representative. When you're ready to use them in a conversation with your parent, start with a small issue first.

You may also want to keep a cheat sheet on an index card in your wallet, in your car's glove box, near the phone, or next to the computer where you most often check your e-mail.

Remember too that with any communication, it's important to think about what you want the results to be, and then to move forward with confidence in your right to ask for and achieve them. That means paying attention to your eye contact, posture, voice tone, volume, and inflection.

You can use the word BELL to help you remember the following elements of clear communication:

- ◊ Be direct about how you see the situation. Try to focus on the facts. "Mom, the last few times we've visited, I've noticed that you've made disparaging comments about my weight—either you say I'm too thin or you tell me I look 'chunky.'"

- ◊ Express yourself by stating your feelings, opinions, and beliefs. "My weight is my business, and I don't want to talk about it with you."

- ◊ Lay your request on the line. It should be realistic and feasible (if you really expect to have it fulfilled). You don't need to explain it. "So when we get together, the topic of my weight and dieting are off limits."

  When possible, present an alternative that's acceptable to you. "When we get together, if you must mention my appearance, I want it to be something positive, like how much you like my outfit." Or, "Mom, if you're worried that when we eat out you might slip and bring up my weight, we can always do something that doesn't involve food. Maybe we can go see a movie together. You love movies, and I've really missed going since I had the kids." (Most people react better when presented with options rather than demands or conditions.) In some situations, if you're open to suggestions about how to solve an issue, you might ask the other person what he thinks a mutually agreeable result might be. Involving him in the process might make it easier for him to meet your request without feeling bad or like you *made* him do something.

◊ Lay the reward on the line too. "If we stay away from the subject of my weight when we get together, it'll make our time together much more enjoyable for both of us."

Adding a "thank you," or, "I really appreciate that you took the time to listen to me (to work with me, to hear me, to take my view into account)" won't hurt either!

Coping with Resistance and Rages

You may need to repeat the sequence above, or some of its parts, several times in response to resistance from the other person. Resistance may come in the form of a "But . . . ," ("But honey, you know I just want the best for you—you're not happy and Bobby doesn't find you as attractive when you're fat") or "Wait, that's not fair," or an outright attack, a nasty comment, or an attempt to change the subject. Don't lose sight of your initial reasons for the communication. You can also respond by validating or acknowledging how she feels and then continue to reiterate what you've said before. For instance, "Mom, no, I may not understand exactly where you're coming from, and I still need you to agree not to discuss my weight." Note the use of *and* instead of *but,* a word which in effect nullifies what you just said. Or, "I can see how it might not seem entirely fair to you. For us to have a good time together, we won't be able to talk about those topics."

Acknowledging and validating how your parent feels doesn't mean you're giving in—you're simply conveying that you can relate on some level. Though you may not agree with the reaction or the degree of the response, if you look at the situation from your parent's perspective (including through his emotional lens), his words and actions may make a bit more sense. Validating how your parent feels may help you stay calmer too. While it's not likely to solve the issue entirely, it may very well prevent it from escalating.

Some validating phrases that you can adapt for your own conversations include the following:

- That must be hard to take/hear/watch/come to terms with.
- I can see how that would be a huge challenge/obstacle.
- I can see how that would be really upsetting to you.
- I would have felt awful about that too.
- If someone said/did that to me, I'd feel . . . too.
- That's hard/difficult/too bad/awful—I'm sorry you had to deal with that.

If your parent is raging or begins to rage during your discussion, you can try the same technique, modified to address the behavior, for example, "I'd like for us to be able to talk, and we can't do it when you're yelling." If the behavior becomes too explosive to continue the conversation, make a statement that you would like to finish the conversation and you'll have to do it when your parent is calmer. Then you should remove yourself from the situation as you would from any other abusive, dangerous, or potentially violent circumstance (Kreger and Mason 1998).

It's not hard to feel like you're going to lose your composure when you encounter a lot of resistance, accusations, or escalation. However, saying certain things to yourself may help you keep your cool (McKay, Rogers, and McKay 1989).

- Getting angry, too, isn't going to help the situation.
- I don't need to prove myself.
- I'm not going to let this get to me.
- For someone to act like this, she must be really unhappy.
- There's no need to doubt myself. I know what's best for me.
- I don't like how he's acting and it's not effective, but he's using the only problem-solving skills he knows.
- I don't have to take this. I can withdraw from the conversation at any time.

It's about You

Framing your statements in terms of what you want, need, think, and feel prevents you from inadvertently making accusations against others. Use "I" statements to be direct; they let others know just where you stand. "I" statements keep you focused on your needs, and they make it harder for the other person to argue with you (not impossible, mind you, but definitely harder).

Next time your parent challenges you or invalidates your feelings, try to structure your responses first with an acknowledgment of his position and then with a strong, direct "I" statement of your own, such as one of these responses, adapted from Kreger and Mason (1998):

- ◊ Maybe you're okay with . . . , and I'm not. I think. . . .

- ◊ You might feel . . . when . . . happens, and I feel. . . .

- ◊ Maybe you find it funny to . . . I think it's. . . .

- ◊ It sounds like you think it's not a big deal to. . . . I don't agree. To me it seems. . . .

- ◊ You seem to do things this way. That doesn't work for me. I do. . . .

- ◊ It sounds like you think I'm saying. . . . I feel misunderstood. What I'm intending to say is. . . .

- ◊ Yes, and I have a different perspective on that. We don't have to agree.

- ◊ You may not remember it that way. That doesn't mean it didn't happen, and I feel . . . about it.

STOP AND THINK: Instant Replay

Think of a recent troublesome interaction with your parent. Try to reconstruct the dialogue as much as possible. What did each of you say and how?

Now go back through what you said and see if there might be opportunities to put some of the tools in this chapter to use, should a similar conversation take place in the future. Would you change what you said and how you said it in any way? If so, write how.

A Few More Things

As you interact with your parent and set healthy limits, keep these additional tools in your toolbox.

Know Your Limits

It's hard to appear confident and assert yourself when you're not quite clear on what you're asserting. Before you address an issue with your parent or state your needs, be sure to clarify it to yourself first. What do you want? How far are you willing to go to get it? What are you willing to give up? Are there alternatives you can accept and, if so, what are they? Knowing what you're after helps keep you focused; it will help keep the issues from getting muddy during emotionally charged conversations.

Don't Expect Flowers

As you set limits and communicate more directly, you can't expect your parent to be thrilled about it. Using the earlier analogy, when you stop waltzing and start to tango, or begin to do anything else that changes comfortable dynamics, for that matter, your parent may feel threatened or rejected. He may question your love, your loyalty, your sanity. That goes with the new territory. So it's important for you to find ways to manage your own feelings about the potential rejection. Some of the tools for grief, acceptance, and overcoming guilt covered in chapters 3 and 4 may be helpful in this context as well.

Be Prepared to Pull Back

Despite the difficulties you may have with your parent, you still may have a close relationship. You may talk or visit often; your parent may be the first one you turn to when you have good (or bad) news to share; you may be very involved in each other's lives. But you may find you also have to separate yourself a bit. That may mean visiting less often, cutting down the time you spend on the phone, not sharing as many personal details or as much news of what's happening in your life as you once did. It may mean finding another confidante. It may mean saying no when your parent asks for help during a perceived crisis. It may mean not reneging on the limits you've set after a period of calm. It may mean pulling back from other relatives who are still enmeshed with your parent too. Only you can determine the extent to which you'll need to detach.

Choose Your Battles

As part of their healing process, some adult children of parents with borderline traits choose to confront them. Often, these adult children write letters detailing the past and explaining how it's affected them in the present. Some raise the issue of BPD and suggest their parent seek treatment. There's no right or wrong thing to do. Like everything else we've discussed in this book, you have to decide what's right for you. And you can't expect anything you do or say to change your parent. Given your parent's challenges, it may not be realistic to expect him to read a long letter about what he may have done wrong, and to accept responsibility, acknowledge that he has some troublesome behaviors, and ask for help. That doesn't mean you shouldn't write (and send) such a letter if that's what you need to do. As with any other type of confrontation, you'll want to examine—and be clear about—your objectives, your motivation, your needs, short- and long-term consequences and, most importantly, your expectations for change.

Find the Humor

The adage, "Laughter is the best medicine," is indeed true. Wherever possible, try to see the humor and irony of your situation. Be able to laugh at yourself. Human beings are fascinating creatures, prone to act in silly, bizarre, seemingly contradictory ways, for a variety of reasons. There's certainly no shortage of material!

CHAPTER 7

Reconstructing the Past, Assessing the Present

As you examine your past experiences and gain insight into the dynamics of BPD and how they played out in your family, you begin to understand and identify many things: the *roles* you and other family members played; the *rules* by which your family functioned; *perceptions*, *opinions*, and *expectations* you and other family members held and maybe still hold. Doing so lets you challenge those roles, rules, and the characteristics you developed as a result.

Learning by Osmosis

Having grown up with a parent with borderline traits, some—perhaps much—of what you learned, saw, and were told by your parent was influenced by his emotional temperament. Imagine your parent had diabetes and did a good job managing his illness. Your house wouldn't have had many sweets around; you would have gotten used to seeing your parent follow a strict diet, test his blood, and perhaps inject himself with insulin on a daily basis. You would have learned what signs meant his blood sugar was too low, and you would have come to learn what signs meant his sugar was too high. It would all seem normal, after a while—not good or bad, just the way things in your family are.

Similarly, you got used to having a parent with BPD traits. And these traits profoundly affect relationships. Think of the *DSM-IV* (APA 1994) criteria and other manifestations—inconsistency, denial, projection, black-and-white thinking, difficulty expressing anger, volatility, often feeling emotionally overwhelmed, abandoned, rejected, attacked, ignored, and ashamed. Any of these manifestations, not to mention any combination, can affect relationships and family dynamics in significant ways. And given that you were a child, your parent's temperament and challenges undoubtedly had an impact on how you interacted with others as well.

Playing Your Role

In your family, you may have been assigned a role. You may have been the black sheep, excluded from conversations and only learning about things second-hand. Or you may have been the best friend in whom your parent confided whenever there was a conflict with a relative. You might have been the ally, expected to take your parent's side whenever there was a disagreement. Perhaps you were the fall guy instead, the one who stepped in to fight your parent's battles and communicate her discontent with the person she deemed responsible. You may have experienced any combination of these roles—or numerous others—depending on your age, the circumstances, and your parent's needs.

Absorbing Beliefs

As a result of being involved in the unhealthy and unpredictable ways your parent likely related to others, you may have experienced estrangements, family feuds, or heard opinions from your parent that diametrically opposed your impressions or others' beliefs. You may have watched as family members were worshipped or demonized, or both. "I'll never speak to you again," may have been your parent's primary method of resolving conflict. And you may have been asked to take the same stand to help prove your parent was right. You may have been told that Aunt Thelma was a loon, or that your brother was a freeloader and trouble even in utero, for instance. And after hearing these things over and over, you might have come to believe them yourself. No, or few, questions asked. Even if your experience with Aunt Thelma and your brother told you otherwise, you may have accepted your parent's beliefs in order to get his approval or, simply, because as a child and even a young adult, you think (and need to believe) that your parent knows best.

Putting the Pieces Together

Now as an adult, it's important to look back and, as much as possible, sift through the past to discern your own thoughts and feelings and to learn more about who the people were around you. Aunt Thelma may not have been a loon. Your impression as a child that she was a kind, warm, funny, offbeat lady may have been spot on. Your brother may have been open and generous to a fault as a youngster but grew to be rebellious and sullen as a teenager (after years of criticism and blame from your parent). There may have been some objective truth to the things your parent believed. There may have been little. It doesn't matter. It's up to you now to make your own assessments as a somewhat detached witness who suspends judgment and deals only with the facts as much as possible.

Family Affairs

A family is a system. It's important, as you think back, to note not only how your parent functioned, but how others around her did (your other parent, siblings, grandparents, aunts, uncles, even close family friends, and of course yourself), and what the dynamics were like among all of you.

STOP AND THINK: Family Rules

Think of a few events in your life, such as a family conflict (within your immediate or extended family), divorce, death, job loss, a move, an illness, that stand out in your memory. Write a description of each in your journal, including your age at the time.

Now consider how each instance was handled by you and the various members of your nuclear and extended family. You can use the following questions to prompt you, but feel free to add your own impressions and recollections:

- How was the incident addressed by different people? Was it talked about openly and honestly, or were some of the facts changed deliberately to protect people? Was it talked about with disdain? In hushed voices? With a roll of the eyes? With tension in the air? Did a fight ensue?

- How were you told about the incident? How was it explained to you? Did you receive any messages about how you were *supposed* to feel and react?

- How did you feel? How did you react and express your feelings?

- How were your reactions received? Were your feelings validated? Invalidated?

- How overly-involved or avoidant were members of your extended family?

- What images or scenes do you recall? How about any words or phrases or conversations that stick in your mind?

- Do you see any patterns among the reactions of family members? Do certain people seem to reliably stick their head in the sand, while others seem to elbow their way straight into the center of conflict?

- Do you see any patterns in your own reactions?

Go to the Sources

In addition to your own memories, which may have formed quite some time ago, there are other ways of learning what life was like in your family. Talk to relatives, even distant ones who you may think don't have much to share. They might surprise you with their recollections and insight. Talk to family friends and former neighbors. (If you've lost track of some of these people and want to locate them, the Internet is a helpful resource.)

Those with BPD-like patterns of thinking and behavior have different areas of competence and different responses to different people. They may function very well in certain situations or around particular people and less well under other circumstances. They may have idealized some people in their life and bitterly hated others. Different family members and friends will have had very different experiences with your parent, so it's important to cast your informational net as wide as possible to get a better idea of your family dynamics.

It's also important to get as much input as possible because it will be difficult for you to see all aspects of your parent. As a child, and as your parent's child, you saw your parent from a particular perspective. Your view would have been quite different if you'd been an adult.

You've also felt (and may still feel) a great deal of pain because of your relationship with your parent, which may preclude your seeing or remembering some of the good. Given human survival instincts, and the strong chemical and physical reactions we have to trauma, it's far more likely for us to recall dangerous, violent, or emotionally volatile situations than the calm, peaceful ones (ever heard of post-euphoric stress disorder? While much research is being done on the effects of happiness on health, pleasure doesn't seem to have the same jarring effect on us that pain does). These experiences are registered strongly, particularly when the trauma is inflicted by a parent, close relative, or caretaker—the person/people upon whom you most heavily depend for survival.

As a result, any subsequent incident that even remotely resembles the first triggers strong emotions—anger, fear, sadness—and negative associations grow. This is not to say that your negative feelings aren't justified; rather it's to remind you that little in life is 100 percent good or 100 percent bad (know anyone who thinks that it is?!). In thinking about her childhood experience with her mother, who would alternate between being very loving and then raging uncontrollably, Donna, forty-two, says, "It helped me to keep in mind that my mother didn't ask to be borderline. Whether it was caused by heredity or the environment, she didn't choose it, and she never set out to make my life miserable. In her own way, she tried her best. One of the gifts she gave me was to always encourage my painting. That was one thing she always praised. I'm not surprised that I grew up to be a painter."

STOP AND THINK: Positive Recollections

- Sit quietly and think of a positive memory—however fleeting—that you had with a parent, even one who was mostly invalidating and/or abusive. Do you remember a song, a story, a particular walk, or a gift—a snapshot of a moment when you felt happy, glad, loved, joyful even, with your parent?

- Note what senses get aroused when you think of that moment. Is it smell, touch, sight, sound? Are these sensations that now arouse positive feelings for you?

- Write about how it feels to be able to focus on a positive memory, a positive moment, with your parent.

What You're After

As you talk with people, you'll want to learn your family's history and individual members' experiences with anxiety, depression, substance use/abuse, schizophrenia, BPD, childhood abuse or neglect, abusive marriages, hospitalizations (for physical or mental reasons), and so on. You'll also want to know what your parents' childhoods were like, as well as how others saw you as a child.

The following list contains some sample questions, just to get you thinking:

◊ Why did your family move from . . . to . . . ?

◊ Why was your sister sent to live with . . . ?

◊ How come there are no pictures of . . . around? Or how come . . . is never smiling in pictures?

◊ How come your mother never spoke to (or of) . . . ?

◊ How come . . . would get so angry whenever anyone mentioned . . .'s name?

◊ What was . . . like? What was his/her childhood like? Others said h/she was . . . ; why might that be?

STOP AND THINK: The Reporter's-Eye View

■ Pretend you're a journalist and you were just assigned a story about a family (yours) and its dynamics. As you think about your investigation, what do you want to know? What are the family secrets? Who do you want to learn more about? What mysteries intrigue you? What's the story of this family? What are some recurrent themes and patterns?

■ Decide whom you want to speak with and from what other sources you'll gather information.

■ What questions will you ask?

■ As you investigate, take notes and also write in your journal about your own reactions to the project.

■ Write the story of this family (imagine you have a kind editor—it can be any length, style, and format you want).

■ Is the story you've written different from the story you believed as a child and as an adult? If so, how?

■ Are there beliefs you held about your family or any of its members that you can challenge now? Are there any beliefs you've held that you can confirm as a result of your research?

Your Role in the Family Drama

Things may look very different to you now as an independently thinking adult than they did when you were a child. As you challenge some of what you previously held to be true, you may realize that judgments you made about people or things you did were unfair. Where possible, you may want to consider making contact with those people, perhaps to hear their side of the story or to apologize or to simply call a truce and try to navigate a new relationship based upon who you both are now.

Ricardo recalls how when he was about ten his mother called the police because she wanted his father to leave (she was planning to initiate divorce proceedings). She told Ricardo she expected him to back up her story, which wasn't entirely true, and say that he'd seen his father hit her. He did as he was told, and his father was arrested and spent a few days in jail. By the time he got out, Ricardo's mother had taken him and his siblings and moved across the country. He didn't see his father for more than fifteen years.

"I felt guilty for years," he says. "I lied to the police, and I contributed to something that caused my father a lot of pain—he lost his job after the arrest. And the separation from him was hard on me. He wasn't a perfect parent, but no one is. He didn't deserve to lose his family for so long. I know I was young, and I was following what I was told to do, but it didn't ease the guilt and it doesn't stop me from wondering what could have been. It's hard to think about. It was tragic, but you can't change the past. You just have to go on with what you have left."

When Ricardo's son was born, he contacted his father to tell him. Over time, the two reconciled. Ricardo's father told him he was never angry at him for lying to the police; he knew his mother had put him up to it, and he didn't hold the ten-year-old responsible. "Having the opportunity to talk to him, to hear that from him, made all the difference in the world," said Ricardo.

As with any loss, you may experience grief over a separation or conflict with a family member that resulted from the borderline-like behavior in your family. You may also experience frustration at not being able to reconstruct the past entirely. There may be many questions to which you can't get satisfying answers, for any number of reasons. The people involved may have died; they may not wish to have contact with you. You may hear several accounts of the same incident and not know whose version is right (chances are good there are elements of truth in them all). With some questions you have, it may just prove impossible to ever really know the answers.

So, in addition to working through grief and loss, you may also need to practice acceptance. You may not like the answers you've found. You may not feel good about how things played out. You may regret things that you said or did or that were said or done to you. But now that you are no longer a child, you have a choice about how you handle these situations from here on.

Will the Real You Please Stand Up?

Who are you? It sounds like a simple question, doesn't it? You know your name, you know where you live, you know what you do for a living, how you spend your days, whether you're a mother or father, aunt or uncle, son, sister, friend. But who *are* you? As the child of a parent with BPD and/or other emotional and cognitive difficulties, it may be surprisingly difficult to answer this question. You likely didn't have much mirroring, or validation, when you were young, which babies need in order to know where they stand in the world, that their feelings and observations and perceptions are healthy and normal. Without that early mirroring, it was difficult to see yourself, to know yourself.

The mask you may have worn might have been the result of other things as well. As a child, you wanted to please. If Mommy wanted a little ballerina for a daughter, you tried hard to excel in ballet class, even though you really wanted to be out playing kickball or at home reading a book. If Dad needed someone to guide him into the house when he was too drunk to find his way from the garage, you probably associated being a good person with downplaying your own feelings and needs.

You may also have served as a video screen of sorts when your parent projected the traits or feelings she had trouble facing in herself onto you. For example, if your mother was frequently angry but had trouble owning it, she may have accused you of being angry. As a child, when a parent tells you you're a certain way or you have a certain problem, well, you usually believe it.

In dysfunctional families of all sorts, it can be easier at times to simply suppress your feelings. They're not often validated anyway, and given the chaos, the rules, the inconsistency, the hurt, anger, and frustration, life may seem a whole lot simpler without feelings.

In all these ways, you may have lost touch with your true self.

STOP AND THINK: Taking in Messages

Think about what messages you received from your parent about who you were and who you should be. Write them in your journal. Examples might include messages like the following, which came from adult children, recalling what a parent told them.

- "You're too smart to be an artist. You should go to law school and practice law. If you still want to be an artist, you can pursue it later. You're a good painter, but you're not naturally gifted. There are others out there who are."

- "I really hope you can afford to eat out a lot when you're on your own—you're a terrible cook."

- "You're really not the nurturing kind. You probably won't make the best parent."

- "You're cold, and you'll never have a good relationship. No one will ever love you."

- "You're selfish (or clumsy, accident-prone, sickly)."

- "You're just like me."

- "You're nothing like me."

- "You're a slut."

Where and how did you learn the messages you received? To what extent do you believe them? Do you find them difficult to change, even when you know they're not true?

Remember, the messages you received didn't have to be as direct as an explicit statement. You picked up signals from how others treated you, from their body language, from what you overheard them say to others, and so on. If you got the message that you were a cold person, for instance, you may not be able to recall a specific time when someone told you that you were cold. You absorbed the message in other ways.

You're in There, Somewhere

A fundamental skill for surviving a parent with borderline traits is sifting. Think of the process of panning for gold. You scoop the pan in a stream and pull up a lot of slimy rocks and mud. Shake your pan (gently), though, and the muck and pebbles fall through. You're left with, hopefully, nuggets of gold and other minerals (what's left may not seem like all gold to you, but all minerals have valuable properties). In the past few chapters, you've been starting to go through much the same process. Your authentic self is the gold and minerals. The muck, mud, slime, and pebbles are the guilt, blame, criticism, anger, resentment, fears, and projections you have lived with that sift out as you shake the pan. The questions and exercises that follow will help you isolate those valuable nuggets of gold and other natural resources.

The sifting process doesn't happen all at once (it's not something you can start and finish using an exercise in this, or any, book in an evening), but rather it happens little by little, over time. One day you might remember that you used to love pistachio ice cream, but you never ate it at home or ordered it in restaurants because your father was allergic to nuts and he'd always make some annoying remark. And so you reacquaint yourself with pistachio ice cream. A few weeks later, you might cook a wonderful dinner for a few friends and realize that you *are* a good cook, despite how your parent used to tease you for "screwing up a box of macaroni and cheese." Maybe you decide to get some different cookbooks from the library to experiment. Or you might take a class through your community college or a culinary arts program. Perhaps a few weeks later, you catch yourself singing along with the radio and realize you don't sound half bad. You can clearly remember your mother telling you in second grade that you couldn't carry a tune and didn't have a sense of rhythm, for that matter, either. That was the last time you ever let anyone hear you sing or watch you dance. But now you realize that maybe you can. And even if you're not destined for a career in opera, there's no reason you can't belt it out in the car, in the shower, with your friends or kids.

You may find that once you're open to seeing things, yourself, in a new light, that these discoveries, both mundane and weighty, pop up often and at odd times—while you're walking the dog, during coffee and a chat with a good friend, in the middle of the night, as a result of a dream. You might want to keep a small notepad nearby to record your insights. The process of documenting them may help them become more real to you. Then you can go eat pistachio ice cream, cook a delicious meal, or do whatever it is that will reinforce your insights. Enjoy the process too. Think of this as cultivating a relationship with yourself, discovering new things all the time. It can be exhilarating!

STOP AND THINK: Date Night (or Day)

On a calendar, organizer, or whatever tool you use to manage your schedule, set aside time on a regular basis to do something special—alone. These dates with yourself can be once a month, once a week, even once a day. Use the time for an activity you enjoy (taking your dog for an extra long walk or hike, having a cup of coffee at a bookstore, and so on) or simply to sit and think, to get to know yourself better.

In your journal, jot down the qualities that for you contribute to a healthy relationship. Examples include respect, understanding, patience, support, acceptance. As often as you can, but especially during the time you set aside, be sure to make a concerted effort to foster those qualities in your relationship with yourself.

STOP AND THINK: Shaking the Pan for . . .

The sifting process isn't one you can (or should) force. And the hardest part about it is that you may not realize what you should be sifting out and keeping in, it's so ingrained. However, you may find that once you start thinking about and even challenging long-held parts of yourself, you'll have periods of time where the insights come in quick succession. The following list includes some of the areas to consider:

- your beliefs—about spirituality, material possessions, politics, social issues
- your feelings—what makes you happy, sad, angry, frightened, anxious?
- your opinions
- your preferences
- your interests
- your priorities (and, likewise, your obligations). What things do you do because you feel you *should* do them; which do you do because they're important to you and you want to?
- your goals
- your strengths
- your talents
- your hobbies.

In your journal, write down any thoughts that come to mind immediately that you want to challenge—the messages you received and what you believed. As others come to you, whenever they may come to you, jot them down too.

Note how your views now differ from the views you held before. Write a statement for each that affirms what you've discovered. For instance, "I used to feel self-conscious about my singing voice. Ever since second grade, I wouldn't sing out loud if anyone was around. Now I realize I don't have to sing perfectly, but my voice sounds good. I like to sing. I may even join a community choir."

STOP AND THINK: Inside or Out?

It may be helpful to identify your true self visually and more actively, using this exercise adapted from *Boundaries: Where You End and I Begin* (Katherine 1993). You'll need a twenty-five-foot piece of string or twine and a lot of index cards. Make a large circle on the ground with the string. On the index cards, write your preferences, beliefs, hobbies, talents, goals, opinions, interests, dislikes, what makes you happy, sad, and mad (only one idea per card). For instance, you might write "rooms painted warm colors" on one card. On another you might write "whole wheat bread." On another, "funny people." You might have other cards that read "spend more time with friends"; "read Billy a bedtime story each night"; "visit Dad at least once a month"; "get Billy to school on time each day."

When you've made all your cards, stand inside the circle. Take one card at a time, and if it contains something that indeed represents you or something you want as part of your life, put it on the floor inside the circle. If the card contains something that doesn't represent you, or something you want out of your life, place it outside the border of the circle. If after thinking about it, you realize you really don't like whole wheat bread after all, place that card outside the circle. Cards with high priorities go inside the circle. As we've said before, you get to decide now.

Keep this exercise in mind whenever you're faced with a choice you're not sure how to make. For example, a colleague asks you to commit to helping him with a long-term project at work. You feel obligated to help, yet at the same time, you already work long hours and this colleague isn't your favorite person in the world. Visualize an index card with the scenario written on it, such as, "Commit to helping Roger with his project and working late for the next three months." Do you put the card inside or outside your metaphorical circle?

STOP AND THINK:
What Do You Do to Be You?

Without really thinking about it, you may do many things on a daily basis that give you pleasure, that calm and soothe you, that help you express yourself emotionally or creatively, that help you achieve a state of flow, that sense that you're on a roll, when you're so engrossed in what you're doing that you lose all track of time.

Stop and think about what some of those things are for you. What do you do that makes you feel grounded? Examples might include

- yoga

- hiking

- running

- spending time with friends

- enjoying a good bottle of wine

- taking a bath with essential oils

- watching a football game and rooting for your alma mater

- cooking

- painting

- making love

- working in your woodshop

- petting your dog or cat

- playing squash.

STOP AND THINK:
What Qualities Make You You?

Consider what qualities make you you. How would your friends describe you? Are you warm, funny, ambitious, mellow? How would you describe yourself? Think about it, and write your responses in your journal.

What makes you feel competent? What do you feel comfortable teaching others how to do? What do you *know* you're good at?

You've Got the Goods

It's not uncommon for adults who were raised in emotionally charged, unhealthy, or dysfunctional homes to continue to lack a strongly defined sense of self and to struggle with self-esteem. While you may face those issues yourself, it's also important to consider the positives that have come from your experiences.

As author Wayne Muller (1992) writes in *Legacy of the Heart: The Spiritual Advantages of a Painful Childhood,* "Adults who were hurt as children inevitably exhibit a peculiar strength, a profound inner wisdom, and a remarkable creativity and insight. Deep within them—just beneath the wound—lies a profound spiritual vitality, a quiet knowing, a way of perceiving what is beautiful, right, and true. Since their early experiences were so dark and painful, they have spent much of their lives in search of the gentleness, love, and peace they have only imagined in the privacy of their own hearts" (p. xiii). He goes on to write about how you're likely stronger than you give yourself credit for. Just simply living in your home on a daily basis and surviving took courage, determination, and strength.

You probably learned to be observant, scanning your environment and those around you for cues as to what to anticipate, when to take shelter in your room, when to go out, how to respond to questions. You also likely developed your intuition and learned how to be adaptable, nimble, to adjust to change and chaotic circumstances. You developed resilience and found a place deep within you that allowed you to nurture and protect yourself to some degree.

STOP AND THINK: Positive Results

Take some time to think about the positive qualities you developed as a result of your experience. Examples might include being compassionate, empathetic, sensitive, observant, funny, and able to find humor in dark situations. They might include being insightful, perceptive, fair, self-reliant, independent, kind, a good judge of character, appreciative, able to see beauty in ordinary things or where others typically don't. Write your thoughts in your journal.

Also consider what you learned about others as a result of your experience. How are you a better, stronger, smarter, more insightful person?

Be Mindful of Yourself

Your inner resources served you well as a child, and they likely still do today, even though at times you may feel that they've been tapped out. One way to rebuild and connect with those inner resources is to increase mindfulness or self-awareness. The more you know about how you're feeling, what you're thinking, what you're sensing, at any given moment, the more strength, power, and control you will have. The better and healthier your decisions will be. The more confident you'll feel in your knowledge and perceptions.

Self-awareness means focusing your attention on the present, on what you're doing, feeling, thinking, smelling, tasting, seeing, wanting, and planning to do *right now*. It means being in the moment. It may sound obvious to say that you need to focus attention on what you're doing at any given time, but it's a true challenge. How many times has your mind wandered while you were taking a shower and you stayed in longer than you anticipated? How often have you had a conversation with someone while thinking about what you needed to pick up at the grocery store or what you mustn't forget to tell your son as soon as he gets home? How often do you vaguely feel your stomach growl but because you're so busy you don't think about it or the fact that you forgot to eat lunch?

STOP AND THINK: Practicing Mindfulness

Try practicing mindfulness using the following exercises. You can do them with any activity. These are just three examples to get you started.

Mindful Walking

Walk slowly across the room and notice how it feels as each part of your foot comes into contact with the floor—your heel, your arch, the outside of your foot, the ball of your foot, your toes. How do the muscles of your foot feel? Your skin? What's the texture of the floor like? The temperature? The sound as your foot moves over it? If you're wearing socks, how do they feel on your foot and against the floor?

Mindful Folding

Using all of your senses, practice mindfulness as you fold a freshly laundered sheet. How does it smell? What's the texture like? The temperature? How does it feel against your skin as you fold it? What sounds do you hear? What's the process like of trying to align the corners and edges to fold it evenly? How does its feel change as you continue folding it?

Mindful Handwashing

Next time you wash your hands, notice how the water feels as it runs over them. What's the temperature like? The pressure? How does the water sound as it comes out of the faucet? As it hits your hands? What does the texture of the soap feel like? Notice the patterns of the suds as they form on your hands. Notice their irridescence. What sounds do you hear?

Confronting Vestiges of the Past

Part of who you are today includes those long-ingrained responses to your parent's behaviors. Those responses, those ways of being in and seeing the world are still with you in subtle yet fundamental ways. The following pages are designed to help you continue to identify the areas you want to examine further.

Again, the by-products of having been raised by a parent(s) with BPD or similar emotional and cognitive patterns may be seen in the following areas:

⬦ difficulty trusting yourself and others

⬦ feeling shame

⬦ feeling guilt

⬦ possessing a negative self-concept, including self-definition, self-esteem, self-awareness, self-expression

⬦ difficulty setting appropriate boundaries

⬦ being quick to judge; judging yourself and others harshly

⬦ black-and-white thinking

⬦ feeling out of sync with others

⬦ difficulty regulating emotions

⬦ engaging in self-harming or self-defeating behaviors.

You may notice that you have issues in some areas and not others. There's no right or wrong, good or bad here. And within each area, there's a wide spectrum. You may show some tendencies at one or both ends, or anywhere in between. For example, you may have rigid boundaries, walls up, or you may have very loose boundaries, so that you become easily enmeshed with others. You may see patterns on both ends of the spectrum, depending on the circumstances.

STOP AND THINK: Where Are You?

For each of the following statements within each area, rate how closely you identify—1 indicating that you don't identify at all; 10 indicating that you identify very strongly.

Difficulty Trusting Self and Others

_____ If someone does something nice for me, I tend to wonder what their real motives are.

_____ It takes me a long time to trust someone.

_____ It's hard for me to feel safe and secure.

_____ I often second-guess myself; I feel like I must be missing something, so it's hard to make decisions.

_____ Life seems very complicated.

_____ It's hard for me to accept things at face value.

_____ It's difficult for me to relax; I'm often paying very close attention to who and what's around me for signs of danger.

_____ I startle easily, don't like loud noises, often feel anxious.

_____ I bristle at unexpected touch even from loved ones, or if strangers get too close.

Feeling Shame

_____ If I make even a silly mistake, I feel ashamed.

_____ I feel undeserving of people's kindness, love, affection.

_____ Sometimes I feel like I don't have the right to just "be."

_____ I can't seem to do anything right.

Feeling Guilt

_____ I feel responsible for others—their actions, their well-being, their happiness.

_____ I frequently wonder whether people are angry at me.

____ I find myself apologizing a lot.

____ If I only tried harder, I think I could fix. . . .

____ I sometimes feel like I'm a burden.

____ It's selfish not to think of others' needs and feelings before my own.

Possessing a Negative Self-Concept

____ Deep down, I wonder who I am.

____ It's a challenge for me to identify how I really feel about an issue or event. Sometimes I just feel numb, or the feelings can be so overwhelming, it's hard to separate them.

____ I often repress or deny my feelings and say things like, "Oh, it wasn't that bad."

____ If I don't have the same beliefs and feelings as others, I worry that they won't accept me.

____ I'm uncomfortable telling others, directly, how I feel and addressing issues with them.

____ I prefer to stay in the background; I feel uncomfortable when I'm the center of attention.

____ I feel unlovable.

Difficulty Setting Appropriate Boundaries

____ I see patterns in my relationships—I tend to choose partners and friends who are unhealthy or physically or emotionally abusive to me or very, very dependent on me. I've wondered (only half-jokingly) whether I have a sign prominently displayed somewhere on me that says, "Sucker."

____ I'm a natural-born caretaker.

____ I really like to solve other people's problems—it makes me feel good.

____ I feel better keeping my defenses up; that way I won't be taken advantage of.

____ I feel bad saying no to anyone unless I have a really good explanation.

Judging Yourself and Others Harshly

_____ Doing things exactly right is important to me.

_____ People will think less of me if I make a mistake.

_____ I've been told I'm a perfectionist, and that may be true.

_____ I find that I'm quick to judge others (in positive or negative ways).

_____ I tend to focus on people's flaws rather than their good points.

_____ I tend to focus on my flaws rather than my good points.

_____ It's generally hard for me to accept someone just as they are. I find that I wish they could be different.

_____ It's hard for me to accept myself. I often wish I were different.

_____ If I'm with someone and they do something wrong, it reflects on me.

Black-and-White Thinking

_____ Seeing the gray areas of issues is challenging to me. Things are either one way or the other; you can't have both.

_____ I like things clear-cut.

_____ For a while I'll see only the good in people, but then they disappoint me somehow.

_____ If someone upsets me, it's easier for me to distance myself or cut them off than to try to work it out.

Feeling Out of Sync with Others

_____ I was a late-bloomer in some ways; there are things I realize I need to learn now that others learned when they were kids.

_____ I sometimes feel many years older than my contemporaries.

_____ People have told me that I seem wise beyond my years.

_____ No one really understands me or what I've been through.

_____ I'm different than other people.

_____ I feel like I'm playing catch-up all the time.

_____ I can become highly anxious in new social situations.

Difficulty Regulating Emotions

_____ I'd say I'm a very emotional person.

_____ My emotional ups and downs have gotten in the way of my making good decisions in the past.

_____ My emotional ups and downs have affected my relationships with others.

_____ I'd describe myself as moody.

_____ I wish I could be more even-keeled.

_____ It doesn't take much to change my mood.

_____ I have quite a temper.

Engaging in Self-Harming or Self-Defeating Behaviors

_____ There have been periods in my life where I've been quite promiscuous.

_____ I show my feelings for people I'm interested in romantically through physical intimacy.

_____ When someone suggests I not do something, I take it as a challenge and do it anyway.

_____ I believe in throwing caution to the wind. You only live once, right?

_____ I use things like alcohol, drugs, tobacco, sex, gambling, or shopping to make myself feel better.

_____ I've had a problem in the past with addiction.

Review your responses. Be on the lookout for responses on either end of the spectrum, such as a 1 or 2 or a 9 or 10, because they may indicate difficulty seeing gray areas or striking a balance. You may want to work on these areas.

An Exercise in Acceptance

As you consider the statements above and score your responses you might be thinking, "Wow, I have a lot I want to work on," or "Oh no, I have a long road ahead of me." Try not to think about that now. The first step toward any type of change is acceptance. Acceptance doesn't mean contentment or approval; rather it means that you're choosing not to dwell on the past, which let's you turn your attention toward the future.

Acceptance means striking a balance between ideas that might seem to oppose one other: you're fine as you are at this point in time *and* you have things you want to change; you're not to blame for what you experienced as a child *and* you are responsible for creating the life you choose now.

STOP AND THINK: Practicing Acceptance

Write an acceptance statement that validates where you are now, the changes you've made, and that encourages you to make more. For example, "I have made lots of changes, and there are things I'm still working on. I am where I am, but that doesn't mean I have to be stuck here." Or, "I'm beginning to understand the roles assigned to me in my family of origin and the rules by which it functioned. I realize I no longer need to step into or follow them when they don't fit. I'm no longer blindly following them, and now I see more and more that they can be challenged." Use your own words.

At times the self-improvements you want to make may seem overwhelming; they may seem impossible to attain. But you're not doomed. Maureen, the forty-seven-year-old daughter of a mother whom she suspects has BPD, recalls how she felt in her early twenties: "I would have told you I had an [irreparable] black, hollow space inside me. I thought if I let people see me that they'd find me unlovable. But I'm not so terrified now to be unlovable. I'm more comfortable in my own skin. I've made a lot of changes, and I'm not done. This is where I am now and what I can handle. I've worked really hard to be sane."

PART 3

The Future

CHAPTER 8

Envisioning Change and Breaking Old Habits

In the previous chapter, we talked about the messages you may have received as a child and how you might have internalized them, incorporating them into your own sense of who you are. Identifying these core beliefs is challenging precisely because they help define who you are. It's hard to see them as notions that can be challenged—they just seem like part of you and how you see the world. Your mind actually filters out evidence to the contrary while retaining supporting evidence. This only reinforces your thoughts and perceptions and makes them harder to question.

Challenging Core Beliefs

Let's say you wonder whether you really are lovable. Growing up, you endured much erratic and perhaps cruel behavior from a parent who was inconsistent with affection, raged often and projected her angry feelings onto you, accusing you of being a "bitter" person who caused fights to erupt in your wake. Today, as an adult, have you noticed that you've found yourself in situations where that has indeed happened? Have you chosen friends who say or convey similar sentiments to you? Have you ever noticed that you react to people defensively as though they must be thinking you're a bitter person, when really they may not have any such notion? Have you lashed out at someone because you thought they were attacking you, even though they weren't? Your thoughts and your subsequent actions and reactions reinforce your core beliefs. They act as a self-fulfilling prophecy. They allow you to say, "See, I really *am* bitter."

That's the bad news. The good news is that once you can identify and challenge such beliefs, your experience changes too. As you stop seeing yourself as a bitter, unlovable person, you'll increasingly act with openness and acceptance towards others. People will notice and respond in much the same way. You'll seek out healthier folks to surround yourself with and, rather than reinforce your earlier beliefs, new experiences will help you change them.

It's Really Possible

With negative or inaccurate core beliefs, it's hard to imagine change. It's hard to envision what your life could be like with healthier, more self-supporting core beliefs. It's hard to imagine all that's possible.

But it can be done. You've probably heard that your personality is pretty much fully developed and ensconced by the time you're just a few years old. However, some recent research has found otherwise—personality actually evolves over a lifetime (Helson 2002). Additional research has shown that your thoughts and beliefs have a tremendous impact on the happiness, contentment, and meaningfulness you experience in life (Seligman 2002). So you're not stuck, not destined to be bitter, unlovable, or any other negative self-perception you may hold.

STOP AND THINK: Imagine There's No Limit

Using these categories of responses—difficulty trusting, shame, guilt, negative self-concept, boundary identification, judgment, polarized thinking, social deficits, difficulty managing emotions, or self-harming or self-defeating behaviors—what are one or two specific issues that resonate for you and really get in your way? For example, you might think of the anxiety you frequently feel—an example of a social deficit and a negative self-concept—which keeps you from acting with assertiveness at work. As a result, you've gotten the most undesirable projects when your boss delegates assignments.

Now imagine life without those disabling thoughts and/or behaviors. If that's too hard, imagine recognizing those thoughts and feelings but telling yourself that that's your old habitual pattern of thinking, and doesn't necessarily reflect how other people feel about you. Specifically, imagine the scenario in which, for example, you feel anxious but picture yourself feeling slightly less so and able to feel more confident doing something to change the outcome. Imagine raising your hand in a meeting and saying that the project you were given to manage isn't the best fit for your skills and strengths, and instead you'd like to manage another one that was discussed. Imagine that your boss agrees and suggests that you two talk about your strengths further so that she can give you more suitable assignments in the future.

Imagine what you'd feel in such a situation. Imagine that in spite of feeling quite anxious, you also notice a boost in your confidence and energy level. Do the feelings you're experiencing and the potential outcome seem like motivation to work on this issue?

Do this visualization for each issue you wrote down.

STOP AND THINK: Create Your Vision

Set aside some time alone to relax and reflect on what you'd like your life to be like—the sky's the limit. What do you want to do? How do you want to live? Who do you want to be with? What kind of person do you want to be?

Pick a medium of expression that suits you, such as paint, collage, pen and ink, a musical instrument or composition, or writing, and create a representation of your vision.

The Opposite Might Detract

In your effort to identify and challenge the messages you received and your core beliefs, you might be tempted to do things that are in direct opposition to your parent's beliefs and expectations for you. For instance, if your father wanted you to be a physician, you might rebel and decide to become a sculptor, an occupation your father disdained. Or if your mother told you you'd look much better with long hair, you might have cut all of yours off just to prove her wrong.

Defining your own self, though, and making changes in your life isn't just about acting in opposition or defiance to a difficult parent. Even saying "I don't want to be *anything* like my mother" may actually limit your ability to realize your own potential. Again, no one is entirely good or entirely bad. Perhaps your parent was a good story-teller and adept at handling people in certain situations. By saying you won't be anything like her, you may be denying yourself those opportunities. In a way, you may still be letting a parent define who you are or who you aren't. Defining your own self and making changes are, instead, about being true to your inner resources, your goals and dreams.

Accepting Limits

While the world is your oyster, and you have the opportunity now to define yourself, your choices, your life, reality is that not all the changes you want to make may be realistic or possible, for a variety of reasons. Some you may not feel ready to address, and some may not change drastically even if you give them your all.

Recent research has shown that our moods and temperament do have some genetic underpinnings. Just how much isn't exactly clear.

While some shyness, for example, may be learned, some may be a part of your makeup. It's unrealistic to think that if you've long been a shy person that you'll suddenly feel at ease running up to strangers at a big party to start a conversation. On the other hand, it is realistic to think that you can do things to lessen your discomfort. Maybe you would feel more comfortable if you arrived early, before the party got crowded. Or you could offer to help the host or hostess with some task that would take your mind off feeling ill at ease. You could think of some conversation topics and scan the newspaper for interesting news items to discuss with other guests. A goal of complete change in any area of your life may be unrealistic, but a goal to *lessen* the troublesome thought patterns and behaviors, to take your anxiety down a notch, to feel slightly more confident at parties, may be attainable.

As we've discussed elsewhere in this book, acceptance plays a key role in the process you're going through. That means showing yourself—flaws and all—compassion. It means acknowledging the current situation ("Granted, I do . . . , and I have some changes I want to make in that area") without making judgments ("I *should* have mastered this a long time ago; I'm *always* so inept"). Acceptance doesn't mean complacency. It doesn't mean you won't work to make things different. It means that, here and now, this is the way things are, which is okay.

STOP AND THINK: Find Your Balance

Refer back to those issue(s) you identified in the Stop and Think: Imagine There's No Limit exercise. Write an observation for each one that includes both a statement of the situation as it currently is (without judgments) as well as your desire or intention to change it. For example, "I may not like that I tend toward making quick, negative judgments about people when I first meet them, but I'm more aware of it now and I am going to continue to work on it" or "I may not be the most confident, outgoing, comfortable person at parties, but I go anyway—I don't sit home because of my discomfort, and I'm little by little feeling more confident."

Being Your Own Caretaker

If you had insufficient or inconsistent nurturing from a parent when you were a child, you may still be dealing with feelings of grief, anger, and resentment over the lack of unconditional love. You may still crave the love and nurturing that children need and deserve. But it's unrealistic at this point in your life to expect unconditional love from anyone other than yourself. Certainly, you should expect—you deserve—love and nurturing from those close to you (as well as companionship, respect, support, validation, patience, and acceptance), but truly unconditional love and selfless nurturing—it's no one's responsibility but your own to provide now.

How to Nurture Yourself

You may not have had a good role model for learning how to nurture yourself, but you may feel quite comfortable taking on the role of nurturing others. Just as you would do for your own child, taking care of yourself in the sense of providing unconditional love involves developing your strengths and accepting your weaknesses without judgment. It involves tapping your own inner resources, as well as seeking healthy external sources for some of what you need. Think of a plant that grows in a drought-prone area, where it doesn't get as much water as it really needs. The plant survives, though, on less water (it may even have become hardier for its experience); it has adapted by taking additional moisture from the air through its leaves and extending its roots further under the earth. Just like this plant, you can seek additional sources of nourishment beyond what your parent provided. You can accept the nurturing offered by friends, by other relatives, by yourself—by accepting yourself as you are and through engaging in those activities that bring you pleasure and make you feel competent.

STOP AND THINK: Go to the Source

Consider some of the people in your life and the ways they nourish you. Who is the first person you call when you have good news to share? Who do you vent to? Who do you like to joke around with the most? Who's your biggest cheerleader? Who helps you feel a sense of peace when you're together? Who seems to really get what you're about, and vice versa? Write down each person's name and describe the ways in which you call upon him for support.

Think of how you nurture others. Make a list of the people in your life that you nourish with your words, your deeds, or simply your company. For each, describe how you offer sustenance. Are you there to listen to problems? Do you celebrate that person's good news? Do you help brainstorm solutions to challenges? Do you validate her feelings? Offer support? Do unsolicited favors?

Go back through your list. Are there some ways in which you nurture others that you could apply to your own life? By way of example, you agree to drive carpool once a week for your friend who has to work late every Thursday. Can you think of a favor you could do for yourself on a weekly basis that would help you in a similar way? Could you treat yourself to takeout on a night you work late, or once a week when you just don't feel like cooking? Could you enlist a family member to do a weekly chore that you dread doing? Write down the ideas you come up with, and then work on putting them into practice. What can you start doing today, this week, this month?

Old Habits Die Hard

Your habitual ways of thinking, of seeing the world, of behaving, are the result of a number of things: the messages you received as a child; the subsequent core beliefs you developed; and the messages you continually communicate to yourself, to and from your own inner critic.

Your inner critic, unfortunately, may have a lot of tools at its disposal to reinforce your negative perceptions, thoughts, beliefs, and actions, including the following, adapted from *Self-Esteem* (McKay and Fanning 2000).

Overgeneralization. Drawing universal conclusions from a single or small (and not representative) sampling of incidents. For example, if a colleague arrives late to a meeting, you conclude, "He's *always* late." Watch out for *always* and *never*. They signal that your inner critic is at work.

Global labeling. Using all-encompassing and/or pejorative labels to describe someone or something. If someone accidentally bumps into you in a store, you think, "What a jerk." Signals that your inner critic is globally labeling include broad, sweeping absolute statements about a person or incident: "She's a bitch"; "He's a computer nerd"; "I'm incapable of doing that."

Filtering. Selectively focusing on the negative while disregarding the positive. (Diane, a woman raised by a mother with BPD traits, likened filtering to feeling like she was covered in room-darkening shades—"the good stuff [light] just doesn't get through. You have to really be more like light-filtering shades, and let at least as much of the good in as the bad.") Signals of filtering include self-deprecating statements and minimizing accomplishments. "Oh, it was nothing"; "It really wasn't that big a deal."

Polarized thinking. Seeing things in all-or-nothing, black-and-white terms and categories: Life is fantastic, or it's terrible. You need to do things just right or you're no good. Signals of polarized thinking include words such as "always" and "never," "can" and "can't," "should" and "shouldn't," "all" or "none," and hyperbolic phrases like, "It's the best," "It's the worst," "You're the greatest," or "He's a terrible person."

Personalization. Thinking (assuming) that everything has to do with you. The budget for a program you oversee at work is cut, and you believe that your boss is trying to send you a message about the quality of your work. Signals include frequently asking, "Are you angry at me?", "Did I do something wrong?" and/or feeling that things are your fault or directed at you when they're not.

Control fallacies. Feeling like you have complete responsibility for everyone and everything and/or feeling like you have no control, as if you're a victim of circumstance. You notice tensions rising during a dinner at a restaurant with your borderline parent, and so you feel you have to appease him by agreeing to stay longer, and you pick up the tab. Signals include feeling guilty or victimized, frequently apologizing for letting others down.

Catastrophizing. Expecting the worst to happen. You're on guard against the worst possible outcome and assume that crises will ensue. Your boyfriend is late coming over one night, and you start thinking that he must have been in an accident or cheating on you. Signals include asking, "But

what if . . . ?" and fatalistic statements such as, "I don't know how I'll survive if that happens" or "I'll lose absolutely everything."

Emotional reasoning. Assuming "feelings equal facts" (Kreger and Mason
1998), that things are the way you feel about them. If you *feel* unworthy
of praise from your spouse, you assume that you truly don't deserve it.
Signals include a changing self-concept based on temporary conditions
such as mood and emotions, acting on an emotion and then discovering
your feelings and impressions weren't really based on the truth after all.

STOP AND THINK: Challenge the Critic

Consider which of the cognitive distortions above your inner critic might
use to maintain the status quo. For each one, write a recent example of
the critic at work. For instance, if your son chose to watch TV instead of
doing his homework first, you might have thought or said, "Michael never
does his homework when he's supposed to," when really there have only
been a couple of times when he hasn't.

Now challenge the distortion and rewrite the statement. You can do
this by asking yourself if it's *really* true. Are there exceptions? Might there
be another way to look at the issue? Could you have made an incorrect
assumption? Using the previous example, you might instead think or say,
"Michael usually does his homework before he turns on the TV. I wonder
if something is bothering him...Maybe he's tired and needs to relax first."

Develop your own list of responses to the critic, affirmations that
you can repeat whenever you catch yourself in a negative pattern of thinking. Here are a few examples to prompt your list:

- I don't *always* do anything; there are exceptions.

- I don't *never* do or not do anything; there are exceptions.

- It's not fair to make assumptions; I need to find out the facts
  first.

- Everyone makes an isolated mistake or two.

- Come to think of it, I could just as easily choose to see the glass
  half full instead of half empty.

- Because I feel a certain way about something doesn't make it
  absolutely true. Feeling and being are two different things.

■ It's not always about me. People have their own reasons for doing what they do—I don't have to take it personally all of the time.

■ It's not the end of the world. I'll find a solution.

Planning Your Work

Now that you're becoming increasingly aware of the cognitive distortions that reinforce the issues and patterns you've identified, the next step is to prioritize how you want to address them. It bears repeating here that change occurs slowly over time, and that you can't expect to break every long-ingrained pattern overnight. Isolating particular patterns and focusing on them will help you make real and lasting change.

In deciding what habits you want to challenge and change first, you might consider several factors. First and foremost, if you're engaging in self-harming or self-defeating behaviors that are endangering your life or your health, you should place those issues toward the top of your list. If you don't feel physically well or you're not safe, it's going to be that much harder to do the introspective work you want to do. By the same token, it can be extremely frightening and difficult to think of letting go of behaviors or thought patterns that you've come to lean on. If you've identified self-harming or self-defeating behaviors as areas for improvement, it might prove helpful to seek professional help as you work through them.

Next, you might want to examine the beliefs and behaviors that interfere with your quality of life, that is, your career, family, friendships, your financial situation, housing. If, for instance, you've identified that you tend to judge others quickly and somewhat harshly, and you've noticed that your two children are acting in ways similar to how you responded to your own parent when you were a child, you might be motivated to make some changes. If feelings of anxiety are hindering your career advancement, and it's affecting your salary and therefore your ability to buy the new car you desperately need, then anxiety might be where you want to focus. If your difficulty in trusting people is affecting your dating life and you want to find a partner, you might choose to work first in that area.

Ultimately, you want to prioritize the steps toward what psychologist Abraham Maslow (1998) called *self-actualization,* or the ability to reach your potential. These steps include the issues that prevent you from being who you could be, from finding happiness and meaning in life. What's getting in your way?

There's no right or wrong way to set your priorities. Certainly, it might be better not to choose the hardest to change, most entrenched belief or behavior first. In trying to change something you're not ready to give up, you may unwittingly set yourself up for failure. And remember that focusing on one area doesn't mean you're completely excluding others. You can take baby steps with other issues as well. The choices are yours to make.

STOP AND THINK: Prioritize

In your journal, prioritize the work you want to do. What belief(s) or behavior(s) do you want to address first? Have you discussed them with your therapist? Are you in agreement on your priorities?

Getting to Work

One of the first steps toward change is understanding. Why did you develop the beliefs and/or behaviors you plan to challenge? As the child of someone with BPD-like traits, you likely had some very valid reasons.

Maureen, struggled with painful shyness as an adult. When asked where she thinks it came from, she responds, "I think shyness comes from not being allowed to speak your mind. I was always afraid if I drew attention to myself that I'd get raged at. I'd also get spanked and slapped, but the raging was more damaging. Walking on eggshells—I think that's what makes you shy."

Maureen also says she has a streak of perfectionism. Her thoughts on its origins? She remembers playing the guitar as a child and making up a song. "Who do you think you are?" her mother asked when Maureen excitedly and proudly played it for her. "Why don't you learn how to *play* the thing first and save being fancy for later?" There were other similar incidents too.

"Now, I either have to do something perfectly, or I can't do it at all," Maureen says. "I still have some black-and-white thinking about this. On the one hand, I say to myself, 'You're pond scum.' On the other, 'You have to be perfect.'"

Maureen's experience shows not only where certain beliefs and behaviors come from but also how a cognitive distortion, black-and-white thinking, exacerbates tendencies toward perfectionism.

STOP AND THINK: Looking at Origins

Where do you think the negative thoughts and behaviors you've identified come from? Can you see connections between them and your early childhood experiences? Can you see how your inner critic and adulthood experiences have helped to reinforce them? Write about your observations, without judging yourself.

In addition to your inner critic, what reinforces your negative beliefs and behaviors? Donna, forty-two, believes fear of the unknown may play a role: "It's very difficult to think of your life, of yourself, without these things, since they've become a part of you. Sometimes you just have to force yourself to do something you don't want to do. It's scary to have to try to interpret things in a different way. It's like you have a new identity. You don't know who you are without the pain. Who do you become? Who is Donna without the pain of childhood? Am I just an ordinary person then?"

STOP AND THINK: Examining Reinforcement

What do you think reinforces some of the negative beliefs and behaviors you've identified? Even though these beliefs and behaviors have likely gotten in your way, consider how they may have made you feel comfortable. Did they seemingly protect you from being hurt by others? From rejection? From taking responsibility for shoring up your self-esteem? Now think about what you stand to gain by letting go of them. Is the fear or uncertainty you may feel now worth the potential rewards?

One of the major issues Donna works to overcome is seeing the world in rejection mode, ready to assume that she's being snubbed, excluded, or talked about behind her back. This has affected her self-esteem, reinforced her shyness, and made it more difficult to meet and trust others. Her outlook has affected her ability to get a job. She took each unsuccessful attempt personally, and it didn't take long before she was paralyzed and unable to think of going to yet another interview. Still, she knew she had to find a way to do it. Her husband had been shouldering their financial obligations alone and, even though he didn't complain, Donna felt that it was unacceptable over the long-term; she wanted to contribute her share.

STOP AND THINK:
What Are the Consequences?

What are the consequences, direct and indirect, of the negative beliefs and behaviors you engage in? How do you feel about the consequences? Are they motivation to change?

Taking Small Steps

Once Donna decided she needed to get out of "rejection mode," she did a few things. First, she saw a psychiatrist, who prescribed medication for her anxiety. (This book neither endorses nor discourages the use of psychiatric medications; this is your decision, to be undertaken in conjunction with your medical and mental health care partners.) She also addressed her anxiety and specific job-related issues with her therapist. She took a one-day course on interview skills to increase her comfort level, and, perhaps most importantly, she continues to make it a point to reframe her thinking.

"I finally figured out that if I was going to overcome this, there was no other way than making myself look at things without the rejection paradigm," she says. "If I lost a friend [she'd recently lost a friend to cancer], I was going to have to look at it as 'this happens to people,' and it is no fault of my own. If I didn't get a job, I was going to have to look at it as a numbers game—you have to be rejected so many times before you get a job. Everybody has interviews and doesn't get the job." Instead of looking at her experiences as rejecting, she chose to see them as a normal part of life. "It's depersonalizing it," she adds. "It's the only way to do it. I still struggle with fear of rejection; it takes a lot of effort to counter. I feel like I have two choices: Live like that for the rest of my life or try to overcome it. If not now, when?"

In spite of her shyness and perfectionism, Maureen applied to and enrolled in a graduate program. She managed depression and other unhealthy thought patterns through counseling, yoga, weight training, and swimming (even though she was told by her mother with BPD that she was an "accident prone" child, and says she was never really athletic before). She went on to become a speech pathologist and joined a private practice. She says, "That was a turnaround for me, to be dealing with human beings every day. It was like therapy for me; in some ways it was healing. I found it to be desensitizing for the shyness. People say I seem normal and healthy, but I know how scared I still am on the inside. It still takes a lot of work." As for her perfectionism, she says, "I allow myself to be more average now.

I can do things and feel okay if they're not just perfect. I keep telling people that my middle-aged goal is to become mediocre."

Start small. Even with the toughest issues, there's always a first step. It can be as seemingly simple as buying a book to learn more about an issue (like you've already done with this book) or visiting a Web site to learn more about something you want to pursue. Give yourself credit for your effort, no matter how inconsequential it might seem to you.

STOP AND THINK: Strategic Steps

What are some small, realistic steps you can take to make changes in the area(s) you've identified? Brainstorm to come up with ideas, on your own or with a therapist or close friend, and write them down.

Think *specifically* about how you will integrate these steps into your life, say, later today or tomorrow. Commit these plans to paper and, if applicable, add them to your calendar or organizer.

Internalizing Change

It's one thing to know in your mind that you deserve to move toward the life you want. It's quite another to *feel* it, and to know it so well that you take action. There's no better way to internalize new and healthier beliefs and behaviors than repetition. That means practice, practice, practice. And then more practice. It means not waiting until you feel better, or ready to make a change, before taking the first step.

Imagine that you're not a morning person at all, but you want to be more productive so you decide you're going to try to wake up earlier. You set your alarm for 7 A.M., about an hour earlier than normal. The alarm goes off and you're tempted to hit the snooze button, thinking that it will be easier to get up in half an hour or an hour, after you're feeling more rested. In fact, if you get yourself up and moving, start brewing some coffee and take a shower, you'll probably feel wide awake much sooner. And you'll have added time to your day and feel good about how you stuck to your objective. Success builds on itself, and many—not all—subsequent days will be easier. Soon you might even find yourself waking up a minute or two *before* 7 A.M., prior to your alarm.

STOP AND THINK: Chronicling Change

Be sure to track your reactions—thoughts, emotions, changes in your outlook and behavior—and your successes and challenges in your journal. Note whether and how you see changes in how others respond to you as well.

CHAPTER 9

Trust Yourself, Set Boundaries, Build Self-Esteem

The concepts covered earlier in this book—overcoming grief, dealing with anger, squelching guilt, communicating assertively and setting limits with your parent, unearthing your true self, and identifying the healthy changes you want to make—lay the foundation for three powerful tools: trusting yourself, setting boundaries, and building self-esteem. These three tools are interwoven; if you have trouble with any one, it's hard to master either of the remaining two. Though not easy, they're worth developing, for together they allow you to live a life that's true to who you are; that's safe, healthy, and rewarding.

Trusting Yourself

Adult children raised by a parent with BPD or its traits likely have a hard time trusting their own perceptions, their own judgment, their emotions, and knowing what's normal. This has its roots in several childhood experiences, including the lack of validation for your emotions and perceptions. Instead of confirming your emotions by showing you (comforting you, hugging you, nodding empathically), or telling you that you behaved perfectly appropriately for the situation, your parent may have discounted or disregarded your emotions or guided you to change your reaction to meet his own needs. If, for example, you fell off your bike as a young child and cried out of pain and fear, your parent may have laughed at your reaction and told you not to act like such a baby. You learned that your feelings and your visible reactions were wrong.

You may also have lived with chaos and inconsistency. There were likely few constants; it was hard to feel confident in your own beliefs and impressions because they were continually challenged and shaken.

Your parent also may not have encouraged you to explore, to play, to satisfy your curiosity, or to take risks. You likely weren't pushed to see that you could try something and succeed—or fail—and that you'd be fine in the end. While you may have learned to be very independent and self-reliant, you probably weren't pushed to test your limits, to see what you could and couldn't do. And so you learned not to trust your own abilities and resources.

You also may have learned that you had to have proof of your impressions and feelings. It may not have been enough to say, "I feel sick"; you had to have a fever or be vomiting in order to be believed. It may not have been enough to say, "I was late because my friend's car broke down"; you had to somehow show that it indeed happened. You learned that your opinions and perceptions, on their own merit, didn't stand.

In many ways, even though you may have grown up before your time because you were a parentified child, you may be feeling like you're behind in some areas, that you don't know or never learned some of the things that others did. You may not have learned to drive when others did, not attended college when others did. You may have a hard time knowing what's normal or right with respect to everything from how to organize a linen closet or pantry to how to act in certain social situations. You may not trust your own instincts in any of these areas.

Emily, twenty-six, recalls her first job with a large corporation. Before a meeting one day, she approached a coworker and told her she didn't think her suit was very flattering, that it was a color that made her look drab and it accentuated her hips. Emily recalls, "I honestly thought I was being helpful and friendly by talking to her about her appearance. But the look on her face told me I'd really screwed up. I was so embarrassed and ashamed once I realized that I was totally out of line. And then I was angry. Angry mostly at myself for not realizing, but also angry at my parents for not having taught me some really simple social conventions."

As the adult child of a parent with BPD, you may also have trouble making decisions. Choices are difficult to make when you're not sure how you really feel about something. If you're not in touch with your emotions, if you tend to be risk-aversive and very cautious, you ultimately may not trust yourself to make the right choice.

What's Normal, Anyway?

It's important to remember that in most situations, there isn't one absolute right or normal way to act. Decisions are rarely irreversible, and most of the time, they don't have dire consequences. Typically, there are opportunities to reassess and take a different path. Most people, too, will understand if you tell them you've reconsidered and need to change your initial decision. Little in life is set in stone.

Instead of asking yourself, "What is normal?", reframe the question, suggests Steven Farmer, in *Adult Children of Abusive Parents*. Try "What is functional?" instead. What will get the job done? Will it hurt me, or others? Is it practical, realistic? Focusing on functionality gets you away from externally imposed standards of normalcy, a very relative and loaded, and therefore somewhat meaningless, term (Farmer 1989, p. 113).

Following Your Feelings

Your intuition will go a long way in helping you know how to make the best choices—you have to trust it. As a result of your childhood experience in a chaotic, emotionally charged and challenging environment, you very likely developed a keen sensitivity and awareness of your surroundings and the intentions of others. You're probably a better judge of character than you think, if you allow yourself to listen to your gut reaction. Whether you refer to intuition as a little voice inside of you, following your heart, trusting your gut, following your instincts, your sixth sense, or "just a feeling," heed it. You do have the inner knowledge you need to make good decisions, even if you doubt it.

STOP AND THINK: How Do You Know?

What are your ways of knowing? Try to notice what inputs or signals you take in from others and your environment.

How do you interpret what these signals mean? For example, do you feel these signals physically, knowing something is right or wrong for you by whether you feel tension (or a lack of tension) in your body?

What gets in the way of knowing? Do you doubt what you feel and think? Second-guess yourself? Judge your reactions and then discount them? Are there times when you're even more vulnerable to this tendency? Have you noticed, for instance, that if you're really busy and a little flustered that it's harder to come to a decision? What if you're angry? Depressed? Consider the effects of fatigue, drugs and alcohol, being hungry or uncomfortably full, of noise, or of strong emotions.

STOP AND THINK: What You Know

Think of a time where you just knew something, about a decision you needed to make that involved a person or a situation, and you made your choice accordingly. How did you know? How did you feel about what you knew? What was your degree of confidence that you were making a good decision? What were the consequences of following your intuition or gut?

Now think of a time where you didn't follow your instincts. Why didn't you? What were the consequences? How did you feel?

Reality Check

Particularly in the area of playing catch up on social and other life skills, you can draw on plenty of resources to learn what's functional, what others tend to do, and what's healthy for you.

You can ask trusted friends, relatives, or a therapist for a reality check of your own perceptions. Doing so doesn't obligate you to take their advice or adopt their methods or views, but it can prompt you to consider a new perspective or see an opportunity or solution that you might otherwise not have. Others' input may simply provide you with some encouragement and validation of your own impressions and give you added confidence to act.

Support groups and self-help books or tapes are other resources you can draw on to see how others do things and to learn what may work for you. Ian, forty-four, the son of a mother with the traits of BPD, says there have been times where he's felt like he was missing important information in his life. "But I never just say, 'Oh no, I don't know what to do.' Instead I'd tell myself, 'I'm going to learn how to do this.' I think education—of all kinds, life skills and academics—is learning how to learn. My father taught me to question things and learn things for myself. I try to ask questions, read all kinds of books, practice new skills—whatever it takes."

STOP AND THINK: A Taste of Reality

- For what kinds of issues and situations have you felt you needed a reality check?

- Think about the resources you turn to when you need a reality check. Whom or what do you look to?

- What have the results been when you've sought input? Have you felt more confident? Relieved at having shared your impressions with someone else? Write about your feelings, both before and after.

Bolstering Boundaries

Your boundaries are where you end and another begins. They're akin to the membrane around a cell that lets in water and other nutrients the cell needs and keeps out toxins by adapting its permeability according to its needs and external conditions. You too can adapt the permeability of your boundaries, deciding how much of others' issues, wants, and needs you want to accept and what you want to keep out. When setting boundaries, it's important that they be neither too rigid nor too permeable. It's also helpful to remember that boundaries will be easier to maintain with some people in your life than with others.

Setting Healthy Boundaries

Healthy boundaries do a variety of good things. They can protect you emotionally, physically, spiritually, financially, and professionally. Healthy boundaries make it easier for you to ask for what you need and state how you feel. They allow you to make deliberate, conscious decisions about what you want and don't want in your life. They help you accept rejection; as you learn to respect others' boundaries, you're more able to depersonalize negative responses. Your boundaries keep you from meddling in others' affairs or invading their physical or emotional space.

Without trust and faith in yourself, it's hard to maintain healthy boundaries. Your boundaries may instead be very fluid and random, alternating between being too strong or too weak. You may not know why, but you won't feel secure or at ease with yourself or with others. Unhealthy boundaries impinge on your ability and willingness to trust.

Reaching Out and Letting In

Boundaries aren't just about saying no or keeping people out; they allow you to say yes as well, to those things and people you want to let in. It may seem ironic, but good boundaries actually enhance intimacy and relationships. They allow you to reach out to others without feeling threatened or fearful of being engulfed.

It's only because of his healthy boundaries that Ian is able to maintain a relationship with his mother. His greatest challenge, he says, was trying to find a balance between feeling like he needed to take care of her and wanting to completely walk away from her to protect himself. Setting boundaries has helped him to have conversations with her without getting totally pulled in by the things she does and says, and he says he's even been able to have some compassion for her and what she must be going through.

Children raised in families where a parent has BPD may not have learned how to set healthy boundaries for themselves. In healthy families, children are encouraged to determine and voice their boundaries, and those boundaries are respected. A parent with BPD and its traits, however, may discourage a child's self-expression and boundary setting. Because the parent may see the child as an extension of himself, he may feel threatened by the child's boundary formation and may strictly control it, and the child. Other parents may take a more permissive approach, neglecting to clearly define a child's responsibilities and limits, leaving the child to do his or her own thing. Yet other parents with BPD ricochet back and forth between the two extremes, modeling boundary-setting behavior in erratic, inconsistent ways.

Not only do adult children of a parent with BPD likely not have a good role model where boundaries are concerned, but they may have felt controlled, manipulated by guilt or fear, and smothered yet neglected in many ways. The result? Unhealthy boundaries—and therefore relationships—that are either too rigid and guarded or else enmeshed.

STOP AND THINK: Messages at the Frontier

What messages about boundaries did you receive as a child and adolescent? Try to remember a few instances when you tried to set limits and assert yourself at home. What happened? How were you received? Were you supported and encouraged, discouraged implicitly or explicitly, or some combination, depending on the circumstances?

Looking back, how do you think these experiences affected your boundary-setting skills and your comfort level?

Note the Signs

Unhealthy boundaries and boundary violations may manifest themselves in many, sometimes subtle, ways, including

- ◊ being involved in physically or emotionally abusive relationships

- ◊ promiscuous behavior

- ◊ controlling behavior

- ◊ emotional withdrawal

- ◊ saying or doing inappropriate things; making others uncomfortable

- ◊ assaulting someone physically or verbally

- ◊ saying yes when you really mean no and vice versa

- ◊ feeling obligated to fix others and resolve their predicaments

- ◊ feeling a sense of dread or guilt

- ◊ feeling anger or resentment over a commitment you made

- ◊ a sense of frustration at feeling that you have no options

- ◊ feeling devalued, invalidated, or ignored.

Susan, thirty-four, says that working on boundaries was her greatest challenge. She recalls dating in high school. "If someone liked me, I felt I should go out with him. It didn't matter that maybe *I* didn't like *him*. I assumed my judgment was wrong, and if he'd give me the time of day, I should agree to date him." She also recalls many years of promiscuous behavior and abusive relationships in her late teens and twenties. "I didn't know how to ask for what I needed. I couldn't say no. I didn't know how to figure out where my responsibilities began and ended. I thought I needed to get everyone else's problems straightened out. I'd agree to something someone would ask me to do, even though I really didn't want to, and then I'd be resentful. When I think about it, my family really laid the foundation for me to allow others to treat me the way *they* wanted to based on *their* needs—I had *no* boundaries."

STOP AND THINK: How Do *You* Know?

Think about a relationship where you felt your boundaries were violated, where someone crossed the line. What did you think and feel (emotionally and physically)? What told you?

STOP AND THINK: What Gets in the Way?

Unhealthy boundaries can result from parenting styles as well as other influences, including fear of loss, rejection, and abandonment; feeling unworthy of stating your needs and limits; guilt; a sense of unease about yourself; past physical or emotional trauma, particularly in response to your setting a limit in the past.

Think of a specific boundary issue you'd like to work on with your parent but haven't yet addressed; for example, your mother frequently calls you when she has an argument with her sister, to whom you're very close. She unloads on you, then asks you for your opinion of the situation. Of course, she expects that you'll take her side, and she tries to pull you in, suggesting that you call your aunt to express your unhappiness with how she's behaved toward your mother.

Now think about what's kept you from confronting the issue. Write about the emotions and the physical sensations that come up for you when you think about addressing it and setting a boundary with your parent.

Ian's Story

Several years ago, Ian was feeling overwhelmed by his mother's requests—she wanted help paying her bills after she squandered her small savings, and she expected him to take her to numerous doctor's appointments for a variety of ailments and complaints. She was living in filth, unable or unwilling to clean her apartment. Even though she wanted his help, whenever Ian was around, she'd rage and verbally assault him about everything from his driving to being a "goddamn perfectionist" when he suggested some simple ways she might try to keep ahead of the mess in her home.

After six months or so of enduring rages, feeling angry, frustrated, and resentful, the final straw came when Ian snapped at his girlfriend during an argument. She pointed out to him how stressed out he'd been recently and how he seemed to be withdrawing from her, consumed with his mother's ongoing drama that left him with little patience or energy for anything or anyone else.

With the help of a therapist, he decided to make some changes that took place over an extended period of time. At first, unsure of how to confront his mother directly, he put some distance between them. Instead of driving her to all of her appointments, he became selectively available. If she couldn't find a neighbor or friend to take her, he suggested a taxi. He also called his brother, who lived nearby, and asked him, firmly, to help out once in a while. He instituted a rule that unless there was an emergency, he'd wait at least four hours before returning her phone calls (in the past, he'd call back right away). Sometimes he wouldn't call back until the next day.

The increased time away from his mother allowed Ian to realize how much he didn't want to be responsible for every aspect of her life, particularly since she was abusive to him. He began to feel stronger and, little by little, started confronting her when she'd make a demand or fly into a rage. She still behaves this way sometimes, he says, but the incidents are fewer and farther between, and when it does happen, he's able to tolerate it without reacting. He helps out when he can and wants to—he no longer feels obligated or totally responsible for her care. His girlfriend has commented that he seems calmer and happier, and a few coworkers have even noticed that he seems in better spirits.

Using Enforcement Tools

In addition to the strategies for setting and communicating limits discussed in chapter 6, the following suggestions may help you build healthy boundaries. They can be used with your parent or anyone else you interact with. And remember, boundaries don't only mean keeping the bad out; they help you bring (or keep) the good into your life too.

Distance

You can use the word LEMON to help remember the different ways you can distance yourself from someone who's violating your boundaries:

◊ Leave the room or the situation.

◊ Emotional distance. Reduce the amount of personal information you share. Limit the topics of conversation.

◊ Move out of the house, or away from the area.

◊ On your terms. Visits and other interactions are your prerogative.

◊ Not answering, or selectively answering, calls, letters, e-mail.

Communication

You can use the word NICE to help remember the different ways you can communicate when someone is violating your boundaries:

- ◊ No. Practice saying it. And remember that you don't need to explain *why* the answer is no.

- ◊ I. Express how you feel: "I feel . . ."; "I think . . ."; "I know . . ."

- ◊ Clear commitments and agreements. Strive for clarity when you communicate your expectations and commitments.

- ◊ Enough! Don't hesitate to denounce abusive behavior.

Self-Awareness

You can use the word KISS to help remember how self-awareness supports healthy boundaries:

- ◊ Know thyself. Be able to identify how you feel, as well as your goals for interaction.

- ◊ Identify what you want in your life. Repeat the circle exercise in chapter 7 often.

- ◊ Self-esteem. Valuing yourself helps you maintain healthy boundaries.

- ◊ Support yourself. Trust that you'll make excellent choices and decisions.

STOP AND THINK: Strengthen Your Skills

- ■ Do any of the tools above seem especially applicable to your situation? Write about how you might put them into practice.

- ■ Can you think of others to add to the list? Write them down, and plan how you will put them to use.

It's a Process

Don't be surprised if, just when you feel like you've got some healthy boundaries in place, they shift. That's normal, and even good. Boundaries will, and should, change as your life or the context changes—as you acquire additional knowledge, as you get more comfortable with yourself and with setting limits, as the level of intimacy evolves in your relationships, as your self-esteem climbs, as circumstances change.

STOP AND THINK: Shifting Sands

Think of a time when you modified a boundary, consciously or unconsciously. What were the circumstances around the change? How did it make you feel? What were the consequences? How was your decision (again, conscious or unconscious) validated? If it wasn't, how did you feel and what did you do?

Know that as you begin and continue to build healthy boundaries, you'll experience awkward moments. At times you may wonder if you're doing the right thing. And even when you *know* you are, you may still have twinges of fear or uncertainty.

Setting and communicating healthy boundaries may also cost you relationships. Those who tend to violate your boundaries may be especially likely to be put off when you no longer allow it, or you may start noticing that certain friends drain or upset you or demand more of you than in the past. This could be a sign that they'd been overstepping some boundaries previously, and you're more aware of being treated badly now. While you may miss certain aspects of these people and your relationships with them, rest assured your life will ultimately be richer and healthier without their behavior. And later on, if you see that these people have changed and can respect your limits, you can always invite them back into your life.

Building Self-Esteem

Better Boundaries: Owning and Treasuring Your Life, by Jan Black and Greg Enns (1997), opens with a powerfully simple statement: "You protect what you care about" (p. 9). Healthy self-esteem is a good predictor of healthy boundaries. Self-esteem means you feel good about who you are; it means you believe in yourself and trust that you'll know what's best for you when it comes time to make decisions; it means you'll know (or have faith that you'll figure out) who and what to let into your life and on what terms, and who and what to limit. It means you have a sense of ownership of your life and all of your choices; it means you live consciously and deliberately, rather than being overly cautious and fearful or allowing yourself to be pulled, drawn, or torn by others.

Self-esteem is learned early on. Infants who receive affection and mirroring of their emotions and perceptions begin to feel confident and, despite their dependence, secure. Children who are raised with inconsistent or inadequate nurturing and/or any type of abuse, on the other hand, learn to feel bad about themselves. This encompasses physical or emotional abandonment by a parent, chaotic or inconsistent punishments and rewards, criticism, and parentification, where children are taught to parent their parent and that having or expressing their own needs is selfish, bad, and wrong. These children grow into adults who feel fundamentally flawed and unworthy, like there's something wrong with them that can never be fixed.

Feeling bad about yourself amplifies the hurtful and the negative in your life. If someone gets angry at you, you assume you must be wrong. If someone ends a relationship with you, you assume it's because you're a bad person. You may gravitate toward friends and romantic involvements that are abusive or destined not to work out because you feel like you deserve no better. You may feel, on some level, that you deserve a painful life, or at least that you don't deserve to be happy (McKay and Fanning 2000).

Poor self-esteem is insidious—it creeps into and darkens every aspect of your life. It may contribute to depression, anxiety and stress, physical illnesses, hostility and resentment, unhealthy relationships, substance abuse, poor personal hygiene and self-care, and emotional withdrawal (Schiraldi 2001).

STOP AND THINK: Self-Esteem Self-Assessment

On a scale of 0 to 10, rate how closely you agree with each of the following statements, which are adapted from an exercise in *The Self-Esteem Workbook*, by Glenn Schiraldi (2001). Zero indicates you don't agree at all; 10 indicates you agree completely. As you do the exercise, don't analyze each statement; simply respond with the number that best represents your gut-level reaction.

1. I am a valuable person. ____

2. I possess the qualities I need to live a fulfilling life. ____

3. When I look in the mirror, I feel good. ____

4. I think of myself as a success. ____

5. I'm able to laugh at myself. ____

6. I'm happy being me. ____

7. Given a choice, I'd choose to be me over someone else. ____

8. I treat myself with respect. ____

9. I continue to believe in myself, even when others don't. ____

10. Overall, I'm satisfied with the person I am. ____

Take note of any responses for which you answered with a 5 or lower. Consider how your thoughts and feelings in these areas may be impacting your self-esteem. Write about your reactions in your journal.

A Sense of Entitlement

The term *sense of entitlement* often has a negative connotation, as when someone has the audacity to believe they deserve something that they don't. But particularly where happiness and contentment are concerned, some amount of feeling entitled is healthy. If your self-esteem is low, however, it may be hard to feel entitled to anything.

Jaime recalls how, because of her low self-esteem, she felt undeserving. "It came out in material ways—I wouldn't hesitate to buy nice gifts for friends and family and make donations to all kinds of organizations, but when it came to spending money on myself, I was a real miser. Most of my wardrobe was outdated, but it didn't seem worthwhile to replace my clothes. My furniture was from graduate school (ten years earlier), but that seemed passable too. My desk was a folding table and thrift shop bargain, and they were also adequate. But I had the money to replace all of these things. Slowly, after working on feeling better about myself, I realized that it *was* worthwhile to replace this stuff with things I would enjoy. I didn't have to settle for adequate and passable—I could have a closet, living room, and office that I actually love to walk into."

STOP AND THINK: You're Entitled

Think of some things you can do to show yourself you're entitled to well-being and enjoyment. Be sure to include changes you might make in the areas of material possessions, friendships and relationships, and health. For instance, you might make room in your schedule to spend more time with a friend who makes you laugh (or spend less time with a friend who drains you), or buy a new suit this season instead of just an accessory to update it. You might buy a new bed or paint your bedroom a shade you've always wanted. You might sign yourself up for a yoga class even though the holidays are coming and you'll be spending money on gifts for others.

On Purpose

Self-esteem is also intricately connected with purpose. Healthy self-esteem not only helps you know what you want and need to do, but it provides you with faith in yourself and the confidence that you'll achieve your goal. Likewise, a sense of purpose helps you feel competent and confident. But what if you're not sure about what your purpose is? Chances are it will become clear to you if you slow down, listen to your inner voice, and think a bit.

Have you ever been doing something and been so caught up in it that you didn't notice the time passing? Done something that lifted your mood considerably? Thought to yourself, "Wow, this is really *fun*?" That feeling of immersion, of total absorption in an activity is called *flow* (Csikszentmihalyi 1991). You don't achieve that state with just any activity, and so the feeling of flow is a good indicator that you're doing something you have a natural ability and inclination for. Other indicators include activities that make you feel better, that make you feel sure of yourself, that you enjoy sharing with and teaching to others.

STOP AND THINK: What's Your Purpose?

If you're not sure about what your purpose or goals might be, consider the following:

- What gets you out of a bad mood? Perhaps it's playing music, or writing, or reading, working with children, singing.

- What are you passionate about?

- What would your friends say you're "a natural" at?

- Are there any common themes to your most satisfying experiences, for example, do they involve helping others or expressing yourself in some creative way?

Write about how you feel during the activities you mentioned above.

Think of three ways you can do more of the activities that give you a sense of purpose and move you toward your goals. How can you further integrate these activities into your life?

Should You or Shouldn't You?

If there's one word that will send you on a detour from your purpose and goals the fastest, it's the word *should*. *Should* indicates obligation; it indicates something that's externally imposed rather than freely chosen (by you). *Should* says you ought to be living by someone else's standards and values instead of your own.

Without a strong sense of self, without much trust in yourself, without healthy boundaries, it's easy to let others' values dictate who you ought to be and what you ought to do with your life. On a daily basis, *should* may perch on your shoulder, continuously reminding you that you're not quite living up to what you, well, should be. Do any of the following statements resonate with you?

- ◊ I shouldn't be selfish.

- ◊ I should be a better parent (lover, friend).

- ◊ I should apply myself more.

- ◊ I should do something where I earn more money.

- ◊ I should go home now; she's waiting for me.

- ◊ I shouldn't get angry so quickly.

- ◊ I shouldn't be so quick to judge.

- ◊ I should go to work today—I'm not *that* sick.

- ◊ I should have more patience with him.

STOP AND THINK: Should You

Think of all areas of your life—relationships, your home life, social and recreational activities, work and professional life, self-improvement and creative pursuits, sexuality, political, community and religious activities, finances, your appearance, nutrition and fitness, your emotional life. Write your *shoulds* down.

Now rephrase each statement to a pronouncement that reflects your true feelings. Instead of "I should" or "I shouldn't," try "I prefer," "I'd rather," "I try," "I want."

The Mind-Body-Spirit Interconnection

Your emotional well-being is dependent upon and at the same time influences your physical, intellectual, and spiritual health. Think about it—your mind, body, and spirit are really all part of the same being: you. If one area is suffering, the others are likely to as well. For example, if you're feeling depressed, you're not going to be nearly as intellectually curious; you're more likely to physically suffer from ailments such as aches and pains, stomach problems, and headaches; and you're going to lack some of your usual spark. If, on the other hand, you're happy and optimistic, you'll seek out challenges, you'll want to learn, you'll feel better, and you'll notice your energy level rise.

Your Mind

There are unlimited ways to nourish your mind. You can take a class, learn a new skill, volunteer for a new job responsibility or project at work, pick up an instrument you used to play but haven't touched in a while, or you can learn to play a new one. You can participate in a community band, choir, or theater production. You can subscribe to a magazine in a field you're unfamiliar with. You can do crossword puzzles, join Internet discussion forums, make time to read the newspaper or a few pages of a book daily, or join a nonprofit organization and volunteer your time. Sometimes just resting your body and thinking, processing the events of the day, or week, or year, goes a long way toward nourishing your mind.

STOP AND THINK: Nurture Your Mind

What are the things you do to nurture your mind? What things would you like to add to your repertoire? Sketch out a plan that includes making more time for the things you like to do as well as time for adding a new activity.

Write in your journal about the changes you notice over time.

Your Body

Though much of this book focuses on your thoughts and emotions, your body is an integral part of your journey toward healing childhood wounds. Taking care of it will only support and hasten the trip.

Eat well. It's a common analogy used to teach nutrition to school children, but it's true: What you eat and drink fuels your body just as gasoline powers an automobile. Develop a healthy diet that includes plenty of fresh, whole foods, complex carbohydrates, adequate protein, and reduced fat (particularly fat from animal sources), sugars, and salt. Stay away from diets offering quick weight loss, which isn't healthy, and those that don't call for a proportionately balanced intake of nutrients. Nutritional information abounds on the Internet, books, magazines, and your doctor's office, so if you're confused about what's right for you or read conflicting information (unfortunately there's much of that out there as well!), consult a professional.

Get exercise. Regular aerobic exercise can improve the symptoms of depression. Even if you're not depressed, exercise will make you feel better. It improves circulation, oxygen flow throughout your body, improves clarity of thought, and relieves stress. If you haven't been exercising, see your doctor first and then start slowly. Have realistic expectations. If you've been sedentary, going to a high-impact ninety-minute step aerobics class is likely to do more harm than good. You'll find it hard to keep up, you'll be sore afterward, and you might very well get discouraged. Instead ramp up your activity level slowly—it will be easier to stick with. Enlist a friend to exercise with you, if possible. And remember that exercise doesn't have to mean hours spent at a gym. Do what you like to do. Walking, hiking, biking, swimming, dancing, jumping rope, skiing, and rollerblading all count. Finally, don't expect to see or feel dramatic changes overnight. Like everything else we've talked about in this book, change takes time.

Sleep well. The Sandman can work wonders. Let him. Without adequate sleep, you get irritable and fatigued. Your immune system becomes compromised. Your patience wears thin, and you're more prone to accidents and forgetfulness. Most people require about eight hours of sleep each night; some need an hour or two or three more than that, and some can get by on only four or five hours of sleep. Do what makes you feel best. If you're waking up during the night, or you don't feel rested in the morning, see a sleep specialist. Certain disorders and substances, including antidepressants and other medications, alcohol, and sleep apnea can all affect the quality and duration of your sleep.

STOP AND THINK: Nurture Your Body

What are the things you do to nurture your body? What things would you like to add to your repertoire? Sketch out a plan that includes at least one positive change in each area—nutrition, fitness, sleep. It can be as simple as buying a more comfortable pillow, drinking an extra glass of water each day, or adding one minute to your morning walk.

 Write in your journal about the changes you notice over time.

Your Spirit

Spirituality means different things to different people, whether it be following the traditions of a particular religion, having faith in a higher power, or following whatever it is that guides you toward a sense of both inner peace and of belonging in the world. Some people prefer going to church, while others prefer a walk on the beach at sunrise. Some achieve a sense of inner peace by noticing beauty in ordinary places—in the flower pot your neighbor just set outside, in the deep green of a plant leaf at your office, in the smell of chocolate as you unwrap a mid-afternoon treat, in the crayon drawing your son or daughter brings home from school and proudly hands you. Others soothe their souls through meditation, or down time, even if it's only for five minutes a day.

STOP AND THINK: Nurture Your Spirit

What are the things you do to nurture your spirit? What things would you like to add to your repertoire? Sketch out a plan that includes at least one positive change, small as it may seem.

 Write in your journal about the changes you notice over time.

CHAPTER 10

Putting It All Together

The healing process described in this book is neither linear nor finite. You'll likely never reach a point in time where you'll sit back and say, "Whew, *now* I'm finally done." Rather, the issues you confront and work through will ebb and flow as you're faced with new circumstances and as new people enter and leave your life.

And despite your hard work and progress, you may always feel remnants of sadness or other emotions that run deep. You may have days that seem especially trying, when you'll feel like you must have taken a few steps backward. You may have times when you wonder if you're doing the right things, whether your reactions are normal, typical, or, at the very least, rational and understandable. Those thoughts are indeed normal, and healthy even. They indicate growth. Think of it this way: if you break your ankle, you may forever feel a twinge of pain when the weather is damp and cold—there's just no getting around that. But that doesn't mean your now-mended ankle keeps you from jogging and dancing when the sun is shining.

Over time you'll notice how you've changed. You'll be rewarded when you're faced with a situation you've faced countless times before, but this time you find that you're handling it differently (better) than you did in the past. You'll be rewarded when something wonderful happens and you're able to appreciate it fully, feel deserving of it, and perhaps even see that you had a hand in bringing it about. You'll be rewarded when others comment on how you've changed for the better, how you seem healthier, happier, more at ease, or that there's "just something about you" now that wasn't there before.

Remember, you can't expect your parent to change. But *you* can change, and you will. "I know that I have to work hard and that I'm responsible for my own feelings," says Mai, thirty-one. I don't expect that the world will be rosy or perfect. I know that nothing will be handed to me on a platter. If I want something, I have to work for it. My life keeps getting better and better, so I must be doing something right."

As you notice these changes, write about them in your journal, so you can see your progress over time. Reward yourself along the way too; hard work deserves positive reinforcement. Be sure also to continually assess where you are, and what you want to work on next. Then reread this book or the relevant parts. You'll see that each time you do, different parts will jump out at you, and you'll retain new material based on what's most relevant to your life at that time. It's a continuous cycle of assessment, planning, and action. Each positive change, each success builds on itself, and you'll likely notice that you have more and greater insight each time you set the cycle in motion again.

The Human Connection

Much of the work outlined in this book has been focused on you and guiding you to increase your understanding of your experience and to identify and implement the positive changes you want to make. Yet all the skills you're mastering very much apply to your relationships with others as well. Just as several of the diagnostic criteria for BPD affect relationships, so too do the effects of surviving a parent with BPD. Here are just a few ways adult children have said their experience has affected their relationships:

- ◊ Expecting perfection from yourself and holding others to that (unrealistic) standard too; being quick to judge; judging others harshly

- ◊ Black-and-white thinking that prevents you from seeing people as they really are, with all their shades of gray, their uniqueness and nuances, talents, preferences, and human foibles

- ◊ Difficulty communicating with a loved one (one woman finds it easier to write notes to her husband and stick them to the refrigerator with a magnet, rather than speak to him about sensitive issues directly)

- ◊ Fearing abandonment and personalizing rejection (another woman recalled getting angry early on in her marriage when her husband wanted to go out for drinks with his friends on occasion; another recalled feeling rejected when her husband, after a long trip, was too tired to have sex)

◊ Assuming people are angry at you much of the time

◊ Difficulty with touch, particularly unexpected and/or sexual touch

◊ Being disproportionately giving (not receiving) in a relationship

◊ Feeling responsible and guilty for others' moods and trying to fix them.

STOP AND THINK: Beyond You

Consider how the negative beliefs and behaviors you've identified throughout this book have affected your relationships. Consider your interactions with relatives, friends, and colleagues—not only significant others.

You Are Not Alone

It's crucial not to discount the role that others—both friends and partners—play in your healing process. It's not an isolated journey, despite the fact that it may at times indeed feel that way. "You always feel different," says Ronnie, forty-four, "just like children of alcoholic parents say they feel different. But the truth is, lots of people feel the exact same way you do. Others have gone through exactly what you have."

And even if others around you have had different experiences, they can still help. Your healing process is not one where you suddenly realize you're all well and *then* go out into the world to seek connection with others. It's almost exactly the opposite, in fact. You need connections with others on some level in order to improve, to learn to trust, to be challenged, to have motivation to change, to grow.

"I didn't do it all alone," says Rachel, forty-seven. "I got help from therapy and my sister and my friends and, most of all, my husband. But I do take some credit for where I am in my life and I'm happy with what I have. Although I've gone through some tough times, I've come out stronger and happier on the other side."

"I'm hoping someday I'll truly have faith in my husband's love and not feel like I have to earn it," says Micheline, thirty-six. "He has had a big influence on me. He acts as a good sounding board for me. My best friend—she's provided invaluable emotional support for me. My therapist—she helps me figure out who I am and what's best for me. Another good friend has taught me a lot about boundaries and responsibility, both my own and others.'"

Finding Support

A good therapist is a key part of the healing process (Kreger 2002). Choose a therapist who understands BPD, especially how growing up with a parent with it might affect children. Randi Kreger's Web site, (www.BPDCentral.com) contains a list of questions you can ask potential therapists to assess their familiarity and comfort dealing with BPD. Other ways to find a therapist include contacting your insurance carrier, asking your psychiatrist or family doctor who they'd recommend, and asking friends for referrals.

Friendships—make that *healthy* friendships—are critical to the healing process as well. Friends should be able to share in your successes and failures, your joys and sorrows; they should be able to mirror and validate your feelings, listen, respect, and support you. If you have friends that don't or can't provide those things, you may want to examine those relationships and consider addressing the issues, minimizing contact, and/or ending the relationship. Friends who tell you your perceptions are wrong, who judge you, who minimize your reactions, or who monopolize conversations may not be the best people to spend a lot of your time with. Often people unconsciously seek out friends and significant others that have quite a bit in common with their parent with BPD; these new people seem familiar, and the dynamics are much the same. Unlike family though, you can choose your friendships. You don't have to put up with bad treatment (not that you do in family relationships either!). And if you choose wisely, you can exchange as much love and support among your closest friends as you would in any family.

STOP AND THINK: Make Wise Choices

What are the qualities you look for in friends and friendships? Think of the people you consider your closest friends. Do they possess those qualities?

If making friends doesn't come easily to you, as it doesn't for many adult children, think of some ways you can become more comfortable with reaching out. Write them down and include your plan to put them into action. For instance, "I would be comfortable inviting someone I wanted to get to know better out for a cup of coffee or breakfast. In fact, I'll ask my coworker, Marilyn, to have coffee this week."

Don't forget to write down your commitment to ask.

If you think about it, there are many resources that can help support you and the work you're doing. In addition to a trusted therapist, partner, close friends, and relatives, there are many types of support groups available. Your county mental health program may offer groups for family members of those with mental illnesses, and while Internet forums may not be a replacement for real-world relationships, they can be a great place to exchange information and correspond with others who have had similar experiences. As you begin to reach out, you'll likely be surprised at just how much support and understanding you'll receive.

Seeing Patterns in Intimate Relationships

It's not uncommon for adult children with borderline parents to realize there have been some unhealthy themes running through their past intimate relationships. You may have chosen partners that were verbally or physically abusive, demonstrated the traits of BPD, or had other mental health and/or substance abuse issues. You may have chosen significant others that were unavailable emotionally, preventing the relationship from going beyond a certain level of intimacy. Or, rather than choosing someone based on your own needs and preferences, you agreed to date or even marry someone because that person expressed interest in you.

STOP AND THINK: Patterns

Think about any patterns in your past relationships. Consider the types of partners you've been drawn to, as well as how your relationships have started and ended and how you treated each other. Were most aspects of the relationship reciprocal? What was communication like? Was there any type of abuse to either person? How were breakups handled?

The reasons for negative relationship choices are many. Lacking a good model, you may not recognize what a healthy person and relationship feels like. Or, you may not feel worthy of a good relationship. You may feel unlovable and not believe that it could ever be possible for you to find someone who truly cares for you. You may not have ever pictured yourself in a partnership because your parent projected other plans for you, or projected her own feelings of unworthiness or fears of abandonment onto you. You may have received negative messages about relationships while growing up, such as, "Men are only after one thing," "Women are gold diggers," or "People always end up stabbing you in the back." You may struggle with feelings of guilt for being happy in a relationship. You may worry that if things are going too well, it's only a matter of time before you're blindsided by disaster, so you keep your expectations low and try not to enjoy anything or anyone too much.

STOP AND THINK: Relationship Messages

- What are the messages you received while growing up about love, romance, relationships, sex, and marriage? Write them down.

- Think about where the messages came from (sources might include your parent, family, television and other media, social mores, teachers, friends) and how you came to believe them—what reinforced them and made them seem true to you?

- For each message you wrote down, write a statement that challenges it. For example, "Men are only after one thing," might become "Sure, some men are only after one thing, but there are plenty of men out there who appreciate others for who they are as people, and who want a relationship that offers good conversation and companionship."

- Consider how these messages contributed to the relationship patterns you identified above.

Managing Expectations

The messages you received about relationships dictate your expectations of them and of your partners. Particularly for adults who were raised by a parent who may not have provided much or enough nurturing and affection, intimate relationships may seem a way to finally get that which you have longed for since you were a child.

　　While intimate relationships can provide nurturing and affection, it's unrealistic (and unfair) to expect or demand that a partner provide it—it's something that grows organically as a relationship evolves, and desperate need will actually preclude it. Other unrealistic expectations of an intimate relationship include using it in order to prove your worth, value, or attractiveness; boost your self-confidence; have someone else support you financially or take care of you; make up for what someone else didn't give you; get back at a former lover; or have a project, a purpose in life, or someone to take care of.

Fair and healthy expectations of a relationship, on the other hand, include reciprocity in many areas: support, companionship, patience, partnership, respect, acceptance, love, affection, sexual pleasure, parenting responsibilities (if children are involved), and, of course, commitment. All relationships, whether with friends, relatives, or significant others (coworkers and neighbors too), take a lot of work and dedication. They'll challenge you, and perhaps, at times, scare you. Still, you'll undoubtedly find that they're valuable—no, integral—to your life and well worth the investment. With others beside you, you'll be able to change negative patterns you may not have even realized you'd fallen into. You'll feel more confident taking risks because you know you'll be supported, regardless of the outcome. You'll be more willing to open yourself up to meeting new people and doing things, with a sense of satisfaction, fulfillment, and love that you might never before even dared to have imagined.

Good luck! Please write and share your success stories with us at http://www.SurvivingABorderlineParent.com. Let us know how this book was useful to you, what helped and what didn't.

References

American Psychiatric Association (APA). 1994. *Diagnostic and Statistical Manual of Mental Disorders.* 4th edition. Washington, D.C.: American Psychiatric Association.

———. 2000. *Diagnostic and Statistical Manual of Mental Disorders.* 4th edition. Text Revision. Washington, D.C.: American Psychiatric Association.

———. 2001. *Practice Guideline for the Treatment of Borderline Personalities.* Washington, D.C.: American Psychiatric Association.

Black, J., and G. Enns. 1997. *Better Boundaries: Owning and Treasuring Your Life.* Oakland, Calif.: New Harbinger Publications.

Bowlby, J. 1969. *Attachment and Loss.* Vol. 1. London: Hogarth.

Bradshaw, J. 1988. *Healing the Shame That Binds You.* Deerfield Beach, Fla.: Health Communications.

———. 1992. *Creating Love: The Next Great Stage of Growth.* New York: Bantam Dell Publishing Group.

Brown, N. 2001. *Children of the Self-Absorbed: A Grownup's Guide to Getting Over Narcissistic Parents.* Oakland, Calif.: New Harbinger Publications.

Csikszentmihalyi, M. 1991. *Flow: The Psychology of Optimal Experience.* New York: Harper Collins.

Farmer, S. 1989. *Adult Children of Abusive Parents: A Healing Program for Those Who Have Been Physically, Sexually, or Emotionally Abused.* New York: Ballantine Books.

Finkelhor, D. 1979. *Sexually Victimized Children.* New York: Free Press.

Grossman, R. 2003. http://www.voicelessness.com. Last accessed 4 April.

Gunderson, J. 2002. Interviewed by the author, 7 October.

Helson, R. 2002. Personality change over forty years of adulthood: HLM analyses of two longitudinal samples. *Journal of Personality and Social Psychology* 83:752–66.

Katherine, A. 1993. *Boundaries: Where You End and I Begin*. New York: Fireside.

Kreger, R. 2001. Telephone conversation with author, 19 October.

———. 2002. Telephone conversation with author, 23 June.

Kreger, R., and P. Mason. 1998. *Stop Walking on Eggshells: Taking Your Life Back When Someone You Care About Has Borderline Personality Disorder*. Oakland, Calif.: New Harbinger Publications.

Kreger, R., and P. Shirley. 2002. *The Stop Walking on Eggshells Workbook*. Oakland, Calif.: New Harbinger Publications.

Kreisman, J., and H. Straus. 1991. *I Hate You-Don't Leave Me: Understanding the Borderline Personality*. New York: Avon Books.

Kübler-Ross, E.. 1997. *On Death and Dying*. New York: Simon and Schuster.

Lawson, C. A. 2000. *Understanding the Borderline Mother: Helping Her Children Transcend the Intense, Unpredictable, and Volatile Relationship*. Northvale, New Jersey: Jason Aronson.

Linehan, M. 1993a. *Cognitive-Behavioral Treatment of Borderline Personality Disorder*. New York: The Guilford Press.

———. 1993b. *Skills Training Manual for Treating Borderline Personality Disorder*. New York: The Guilford Press.

———. 2001. Personal communication with author, 31 October.

Maslow, A. 1998. *Toward a Psychology of Being*. 3rd edition. New York: John Wiley and Sons.

McKay, M., and P. Fanning. 2000. *Self-Esteem*. Oakland, Calif.: New Harbinger Publications.

McKay, M., P. Rogers, and J. McKay. 1989. *When Anger Hurts: Quieting the Storm Within*. Oakland, Calif.: New Harbinger Publications.

Miller, A. 1996. *The Drama of the Gifted Child: The Search for the True Self*. New York: Basic Books.

Muller, W. 1992. *Legacy of the Heart: The Spiritual Advantages of a Painful Childhood*. New York: Fireside.

Rubio-Stipec, M., H. Bird, G. Canino, M. Bravo, and M. Alegria. 1991. Children of alcoholic parents in the community. *Journal of Studies on Alcohol* 52(1):78–88.

Schiraldi, G. 2001. *The Self-Esteem Workbook*. Oakland, Calif.: New Harbinger Publications.

Seligman, M. 2002. *Authentic Happiness: Using the New Positive Psychology to Realize Your Potential for Lasting Fulfillment*. New York: Free Press.

Shirley, P. 2001. E-mail communication with author, December.

Silk, K. 2002. Interview with author, 4 October.

Swartz, M., D. Blazer, L. George, and I. Winfield. Estimating the prevalence of borderline personality disorder in the community. *Journal of Personality Disorders* 4(3):257–71.

Weiss, M., P. Zelkowitz, R. Feldman, J. Vogel, M. Heyman, and J. Paris. 1996. Psychopathology in offspring of mothers with borderline personality disorder: A pilot study. *Canadian Journal of Psychiatry* 41:285–290.

Kimberlee Roth is a health writer and journalist. She has written about Borderline Personality Disorder and topics related to physical and emotional well being for numerous newspapers and magazines, including the *Chicago Tribune*.

Freda Friedman, Ph.D., LCSW, is in private practice and a member of the Phoenix Institute in Chicago, Illinois. For the past twenty years, her primary clinical focus has been with Borderline Personality Disorder, providing treatment, education, support and consultation to people suffering from the disorder, their families and health care professionals working with them. She is on the board of several professional health care organizations and has developed BPD programs in New York and Chicago.

Some Other
New Harbinger Titles

Helping A Child with Nonverbal Learning Disorder, 2nd edition
    Item 5266 $15.95

The Introvert & Extrovert in Love, Item 4863 $14.95

Helping Your Socially Vulnerable Child, Item 4580 $15.95

Life Planning for Adults with Developmental Disabilities, Item 4511 $19.95

But I Didn't Mean That! Item 4887 $14.95

The Family Intervention Guide to Mental Illness, Item 5068 $17.95

It's So Hard to Love You, Item 4962 $14.95

The Turbulent Twenties, Item 4216 $14.95

The Balanced Mom, Item 4534 $14.95

Helping Your Child Overcome Separation Anxiety & School Refusal,
    Item 4313 $14.95

When Your Child Is Cutting, Item 4375 $15.95

Helping Your Child with Selective Mutism, Item 416X $14.95

Sun Protection for Life, Item 4194 $11.95

Helping Your Child with Autism Spectrum Disorder, Item 3848 $17.95

Teach Me to Say It Right, Item 4038 $13.95

Grieving Mindfully, Item 4011 $14.95

The Courage to Trust, Item 3805 $14.95

The Gift of ADHD, Item 3899 $14.95

The Power of Two Workbook, Item 3341 $19.95

Adult Children of Divorce, Item 3368 $14.95

*Fifty Great Tips, Tricks, and Techniques to Connect
with Your Teen,* Item 3597 $10.95

Helping Your Child with OCD, Item 3325 $19.95

Helping Your Depressed Child, Item 3228 $14.95

Call **toll free, 1-800-748-6273,** or log on to our online bookstore at **www.newharbinger.com** to order. Have your Visa or Mastercard number ready. Or send a check for the titles you want to New Harbinger Publications, Inc., 5674 Shattuck Ave., Oakland, CA 94609. Include $4.50 for the first book and 75¢ for each additional book, to cover shipping and handling. (California residents please include appropriate sales tax.) Allow two to five weeks for delivery.

Prices subject to change without notice.